Twilight of the Elites

TWILIGHT OF THE ELITES

PROSPERITY, THE PERIPHERY, AND THE FUTURE OF FRANCE

● ● ●

CHRISTOPHE GUILLUY

TRANSLATED FROM THE FRENCH BY
MALCOLM DeBEVOISE

Yale
UNIVERSITY PRESS
New Haven and London

Yale University Press books may be purchased in quantity for educational,
business, or promotional use. For information, please e-mail sales.press@
yale.edu (U.S. office) or sales@yaleup.co.uk (U.K. office).

Set in Gotham and Adobe Garamond types by IDS Infotech Ltd.
Printed in the United States of America.

Library of Congress Control Number: 2018952407
ISBN 978-0-300-23376-6 (hardcover : alk. paper)

A catalogue record for this book is available from the British Library.
This paper meets the requirements of ANSI/NISO Z39.48-1992
(Permanence of Paper).

10 9 8 7 6 5 4 3 2 1

Contents

Introduction   1

1 The New Citadels   4

2 An Americanized Society   51

3 The Management of Public Opinion   74

4 The Defection of the Working Class   100

   Conclusion   141

   Appendix: An Index of Socioeconomic Fragility   145

   Notes   151

   Index   169

Introduction

Amid a fanfare of republican self-congratulation, France has embraced globalization in all its glory. Wherever one looks, from the chronic alternation between traditional parties of the center left and center right[1] to the denial of democracy itself, with the farcical referendum of 2005 on a European constitution, it is plain to see that France has become an "American" society like all the rest, inegalitarian and multicultural. In the space of a few decades, the implacable law of global markets has asserted its authority everywhere, replacing a society founded on egalitarian ideals by a polarized society seething with tensions of every sort beneath a placid surface. The unprecedented social and cultural disruption provoked by this sudden swing has until now been covered up by a patriotic blast of trumpets. But this republican fanfare, though it grows louder and louder, rings ever more false with the passage of time. As in all the other developed countries, the new economic order does not cease sowing division and discord.

How could things have changed so quickly? How could a dominant class, by definition minuscule, have managed to impose an economic model that no one, and especially not the working classes, had chosen? How was this model able to win acceptance so easily, when criticism of a system run by bankers (and the wealthy oligarchs they are assumed to serve) is a commonplace of intellectual commentary and political debate?

All of this was possible in the first place because the dominant class is supported by a large segment of society, namely, all those who gain from globalization or who are protected against its adverse consequences. These people, though they themselves need not be either rich or owners of capital, make up a crucial part of what I call the higher France. This privileged stratum consists of not only the country's elites and traditional upper classes but also the new bourgeoisie that supports them, without whose aid nothing could have been done. Together they bear responsibility for economic and social policies that have plunged a majority of the working class into a kind of insecurity it had not previously known. They are agreed in placing the nation's economy on a new territorial basis, metropolization, that has the effect of banishing the least well-off members of society to the periphery, condemned to live out their lives as second-class citizens.

Globalization has revived the citadels of medieval France. No longer walled cities, they are now modern cities in which a new class that captures most of the benefits of offshore production and free trade is concentrated. Workers in the developed countries, excluded from a broader economy based on an international division of labor in which they no longer have a place, being relatively overpaid and underprotected, find themselves relegated to a lower France, the France of small and medium-sized towns and rural areas. Everywhere, from peripheral France (the part of the country that rejected the European Union by voting no in the 2005 referendum) to peripheral Britain (the land of Brexit), from peripheral America (the land of Trump) to peripheral Sweden (the vanguard of the European alt-right) and beyond, economic globalization arouses the same spirit of populist revolt.

It is owing to this very spirit that the higher France now finds itself in grave danger of losing control over the lower. The Maastricht Treaty of 1992 was the first shot across the bow, the referendum of

2005 the second. The existing order will finally break down not as the result of some decisive event; it will break down as the result of a slow process of social and cultural disaffiliation on the part of the working class. The political class in the broadest sense—not only politicians but cultural leaders, intellectuals, and journalists—now begins to dread the prospect of a modern slave rebellion. For a new form of class conflict, which had long been assumed not to exist, is now plain for all to see.

1

The New Citadels

The medieval citadels are back. In the globalized metropolises, a new kind of bourgeoisie has taken power, without hatred or violence. Wealth, jobs, and political and cultural power have been unobtrusively seized. Although the great divide in French society is often described as a confrontation between "elites" and "the people," the system rests not only on elites but also on a very sizable fraction of the population, a new upper-middle class, which lives mainly in the major cities and which has supported the economic policies of the upper class for thirty years now.

Unlike the old bourgeoisie, its successors understand that economic and cultural domination will be all the more effective as it is exercised in the name of the common good and openness. From Bordeaux to Lyon to Paris, the new bourgeoisie votes for center-left or center-right candidates representing the global economy and resides for the most part in the fifteen largest urban centers of France. Disguised as hipsters, the new gentrifiers busy themselves scrambling for the spoils left over from the modern-day hunt, which is to say the plundering of French society through the imposition of a new economic order, the Anglo-Saxon model of globalization. This radical change was accomplished with little public protest or dissent by means of a contrived opposition between the enlightened and forward-looking champions of an open society and the blinkered defenders of the past, who call on France to take refuge behind closed borders. The voice of the working class, now associated with the camp of withdrawal, became inaudible. The dominant classes, for their part, having now at last disposed of the social question, were free to impose their view of the world in the name of modernity, openness, even equality. After several decades during which the economic and social landscape has been quietly reconfigured, the higher France now lives undisturbed in the safety of its new citadels. If global metropolises are the most visible evidence of this state of affairs, their invisible ramparts—the social and cultural supremacy of the new bourgeoisie—illustrate still more plainly the tendency to associate with one's own kind, known as self-segregation.

Behind the myth of the open and egalitarian society of the cosmopolitan urban centers, then, we are witnessing the return of the closed towns of the Middle Ages and the consolidation of an inegalitarian model of the Anglo-Saxon type. This reality is obscured by the manufacture of a consensual and positive understanding of the benefits of metropolization accruing from the concentration of economic productivity in fifteen major French cities, which themselves may be thought of as constituting a networked society. In singing the praises of "diversity" while at the same time establishing a system marked by deep social and economic inequalities, the dominant classes are able to conceal the bonds of fellowship that unite the beneficiaries of globalization, the roots of a conflict among classes that no one dares mention, and the latent tensions that are bound to emerge in a multicultural nation.

For in these metropolitan areas it is not only patrimony, wealth, and jobs that have been confiscated; it is here that a single way of thinking and talking about these things has been conceived, the discourse of a political system (and of the media outlets that interpret it for popular consumption) that allows the dominant classes to substitute for the reality of a nation subject to severe stresses and strains the fable of a kind and welcoming society. It should be obvious that France is not the land of *fraternité* it pretends to be; but reality no longer matters. Devoid of all collective attachment except membership in its own club, the new bourgeoisie merrily surfs the surging waves of the market, reinforcing its class position, capturing the economic benefits of globalization, and building up a portfolio of real estate holdings that soon will rival that of the old bourgeoisie.

Notwithstanding the protection afforded by the neo-medieval citadels, the executives of the higher France have not retreated from the world. Far from it. The new bourgeoisie openly presides over cultural and political life in the name of the common good and racial unity. Unlike the old bourgeoisie, which was unable to abolish class conflict, it has managed to persuade itself, if no one else, that the ideal of a society without class interests or divisions—what it likes to call "living together in harmony"—is suddenly within reach. In advocating free trade and cultural diversity, it has helped its masters to raise barriers that are no less effective in keeping out the masses than those of the old regime.

The Lie of the Open Society

The bourgeoisie used to stand for class loyalty, self-segregation, rejection of outsiders, refusal of progress. That was then. Today, it no longer locks itself away in its own private world. Professing to believe that social and cultural mixing is a necessity, fully consonant with republican values, its members are more than happy to march alongside their fellow citizens for "change." In reality, though, self-segregation and networking have never been practiced more enthusiastically. Today's amiable go-getters participate directly or indirectly in the vital process of demoting the working class through economic and social policies that exclude the less well-off from the places that really matter, the large cities where most jobs are created. The looting of the private housing stock of the major urban centers, formerly occupied by the working class, has no equivalent in the nation's history. What is more, all this is taking place with a minimum of fuss and on an expanding scale, without the legitimacy of such dispossession ever being questioned, still less seriously objected to—unsurprisingly, perhaps, since the preponderance of the dominant classes in the places where jobs and wealth are created for the most part is also accompanied by the growing influence of these same classes over public debate. The social and geographical gregariousness of the dominant classes goes hand in hand with an intellectual gregariousness that stifles genuine discussion. From the concentration of the winners from globalization in areas of the country having something like a monopoly over wealth and job creation, there arises a uniform style of thinking and speaking, an edifying discourse of benign globalization and metropolization broadcast by the media and repeated by the political class that looks to them for direction. It is futile, then, to expect that any meaningful referendum will one day be held on globalization, on Europe, on free-trade agreements, or on the reform of local governments in France.

The upper classes swear only by the "network," whether the virtual network of the internet or the physical network of the major cities. It allows them to furtively justify the relegation of the lower classes by persuading people that living in somewhere like Cantal, one of the most isolated regions in France, is really no different than living in New York, that career opportunities in small towns and large cities are identical because in each place one is equally "connected." All the vague talk about interconnectedness, mobility, trade, social diversity, openness to others, and so on is a way of obscuring the effects of unequal economic development and a form of regional organization that shuts out most of the less well-off from the large cities. The myth of networked mobility propagated by the media and an intelligentsia with a vested interest in metropolization is cleverly deployed to mask the seizure of wealth: on the one hand, there is the virtual network, a snare and a delusion for the working poor; on the other, there is the real network of their masters, which efficiently connects wealth with a common self-interest. In taking up residence in the major European cities and the regional centers of France, corporate executives and their counterparts in the academy and the liberal professions consciously or unconsciously endorse a strategy of social ghettoization. The same strategy is applied in the "mixed neighborhoods" of large cities, where exclusive apartment buildings for the upper class and private schools for their children are the norm. If certain cultural and political differences still make it possible to distinguish between a new and an old bourgeoisie, both subscribe to the same economic model. However much they may appear to disagree on social questions, both profit from a global economy and its corollary, metropolization.

Sheltered behind the reassuring rhetoric of modernity, openness, and peaceful coexistence, the dominant classes play an active role in impoverishing the lives of a majority of the working class by removing them from the country's economic and cultural centers. In view of the ongoing concentration of wealth and power in the great cities, and the influence of these cities over regional politics and the press (most politicians and media outlets protect the interests of the areas having these cities as their administrative seat), advocates for rural populations, for the small and medium-sized cities and their surrounding departments, have little chance of making themselves heard—and this all the more as the dominant classes are able to achieve their purposes under cover of euphemism.

The upper classes call for equality among the nation's regions while at the same time promoting metropolization and gentrification: they demand greater social diversity but separate themselves from the lower classes by living apart from them; they urge everyone to get along but create a ghettoized educational system in which the children of the poor have no choice but to go to public schools that their own children are able to avoid; they uphold republican principles (and none more resolutely than the principle of equality) but in reality favor inegalitarianism.

The predicament presently facing France is therefore misleadingly imagined to pit supporters of an open society against the supporters of a closed society. On the one side are the new moderns, those who are intelligent enough to perceive the direction of history and generous enough to teach their fellow citizens to see the world as they do; on the other are the new ancients—the backward looking, the unqualified, the weak minded, the uneducated. This way of putting the matter obscures two things. The first is that this ideological divide is, at bottom, a social divide between the upper classes, who gain from globalization, and the lower classes, who lose from it. The second is that the social question has been concealed by a concerted attempt for several decades now to legitimize the economic advantages enjoyed by the upper classes. The open society / closed society cleavage effectively places the upper classes in a position of moral superiority: any critique of the existing socioeconomic system is interpreted as evidence of an attitude favoring retreat and withdrawal from the world that recalls the dark days of the 1930s. In this little game, the working poor are bound to lose. The political failure of the opponents of economic globalism, from the extreme left to the extreme right, is proof of the effectiveness of calculated cynicism.

The success of this strategy is all the more perverse as the open, diverse, egalitarian society that is so much talked about in no way corresponds to reality, and still less to what the upper classes actually want. A globalized society is a closed society in which the combined effects of class inbreeding, residential separatism, educational apartheid, and a selfish determination to accumulate wealth and property have never been so powerful. The picture presented by the fairy tale that has been told over and over again for twenty years now by the media, in which the good do battle against the wicked, could not be more false. French society is not divided between enlightened partisans of progress and their uncultivated and blinkered adversaries. The true divide is between those who stand to gain from globalization, or at least have the means to protect themselves against occasional misfortune, and those who stand to lose from globalization, who are powerless to withstand its merciless onslaught.

Behind all the talk about openness there is a different and rather less comforting reality: the self-ghettoization of the dominant classes, a strengthened system of social reproduction, and the advent of an oligarchic political system whose outstanding feature is the habitual alternation between traditional parties of the left and the right that I mentioned at the outset. By fostering globalism and multiculturalism, the elites have been able surreptitiously to bring about the emergence of a profoundly inegalitarian system, tearing down a system of social protections that has finally outlived its usefulness.

The elites and the privileged classes that support them are well aware that a globalized and multicultural society is viable only on the condition that they can protect themselves from the tensions it unavoidably generates—social tensions arising from a future without any hope of economic prosperity for the working class and cultural tensions arising from a society that has now acquired multiple identities. The guarantees that the elites seek cannot come from a welfare state weakened by neoliberal economic and social policies; they can only come from a strengthening of class self-segregation and systematic avoidance of the lower classes in daily life. Having no real desire to live together (since living together with someone who makes €1,000 a month, or about $14,000 [USD] a year, would mean actually seeing this person in one's own apartment building, meeting him or her on the way to work, sending one's children to the same schools as his or her children, and so on), the dominant classes piously accuse those who lack the means to protect themselves of being responsible for these very tensions.

The discourse of openness to the world and benign regard for people of different backgrounds may now be seen for what it is: a smoke screen devised to conceal the emergence of a closed and isolated society whose greatest beneficiaries are the upper classes themselves. The impregnable fortresses erected in the name of economic rationality so that the upper classes will be assured of having the lion's share of wealth and jobs are surrounded by stronger and more imposing ramparts than the curtain walls of medieval castles. For the walls of money that divide peripheral France from the major cities make it possible to keep out the plebeians much more effectively than in the past. The metropolises of the present day provide public housing in outlying districts for the underpaid immigrant workers who supply cheap labor for the metropolitan economy, thereby helping to sustain the artificial image of an open city. Sixty percent of immigrants in France today live in these *banlieues* of the fifteen largest cities.

It will be clear, then, that the fashionable globalism of the major urban centers has won: it has brought us back to the Middle Ages. In the space of a few decades, a new bourgeoisie, secure in its gentrified redoubts, has expropriated the common inheritance of the nation— jobs, wealth, political and cultural power. What is more, this seizure has been covertly achieved with the aid of a deceitful rhetoric that conceals its true consequences. Class domination must remain invisible. Working-class France must likewise be unseen, and the upper class lumped together in the popular mind with the middle class. The hysterical reaction of academics and the media in France to the term "bourgeois bohemian" (or "bobo"),[1] which reintroduces a class relation between newcomers (from the upper and/or intellectual classes) and members of the traditional working class (some of immigrant descent), betrays their determination to hide the confiscation by the elites not only of a patrimony that formerly belonged to the working classes but also of most of the benefits of globalization.

Hipsters at the Gate

If previous generations of the bourgeoisie lusted after money and power in more nakedly opportunistic ways, the boboized upper classes embody the laid-back style of domination in the twenty-first century. Like its predecessor, though, the new bourgeoisie instigates and supports the great economic, social, cultural, and urban transformations of its time, and again for its own benefit. The upper classes today have seen their income and economic power increase with the spread of market deregulation throughout the world. The real estate holdings they have accumulated are every bit the equal in value of the townhouses of the industrial bourgeoisie of the nineteenth century, but with this difference: there is nothing at all ostentatious about today's bourgeoisie; its members live in what was once workers' housing, in old factories and commercial buildings converted into lofts, in what they persist in calling "working-class neighborhoods." This is a very big difference, indeed the central aspect of the new form of domination. Today's bourgeoisie is the antithesis of yesterday's, at least in the sense that its members have understood that their interests will be defended not through class struggle but through the blurring of class divisions. It is precisely in order to assist this confusion that the use of the term "bobo" is frowned on by the very people whom it identifies as bourgeois. The new bourgeoisie has not displaced the traditional bourgeoisie and the wealthiest families, who still live in their traditional neighborhoods;[2] instead it has expanded into all those areas formerly occupied by the middle and working classes.

No longer obliged to wage old wars, the new bourgeoisie quickly grasped the importance of adopting a new look. The election in the big cities of candidates from the center right and center left neatly completed the picture of a hip upper-middle class devoted to a new conception of urbanism and a particularly agreeable way of life, wholesome, healthy, and environmentally friendly. Paris, the seat of all economic and cultural power, where real estate prices are the highest in the country, is now a bastion of the "left." Although it is the richest city in France, with the highest proportion of executives and white-collar managers (43 percent of the local workforce), more of its elected officials come from the ranks of the Socialist Party than anywhere in the country, more even than in the historically working-class northern region.

Paris is home, in other words, to the highest stage of the new capitalism, a "cool" capitalism that offers all of the advantages of a market economy without any of the inconveniences of class struggle. Posing as protesters at the trade show of the global economy, bobos occupy the upper end of the wage scale; opposed—completely opposed!—to the interests of employers, they hold high-ranking jobs in the strategic sectors of the CAC 40, a benchmark stock market index; scourges of the reigning ideology, they manufacture most of the cultural and media discourse; offended by social fragmentation, they accomplish it themselves through the Uberization of society. Finance is the enemy, but *their* finances are in fine shape, thank you, and their property values have never been higher. Cleverly disguised as hipsters, untroubled by the least moral qualm in the safety of their townhouses, today's bourgeoisie forms the bulwark of the hardest and most unpitying form of capitalism imaginable.

The members of this self-styled "new school," who see themselves as the antithesis of the "old-school people" of the traditional bourgeoisie,[3] call for an open and diverse society—so long as it is more efficient than the present one. Having a vested interest in globalization and its corollary, metropolization, they quite naturally defend their position by deploying the most formidable weapon of all: the law of the market.

Recent surveys reveal that while a majority of the French (almost 60 percent) consider globalization to be a threat, the upper-class population of the major cities tends to see it as an opportunity: 62 percent of executives held this view in 2016, as against 24 percent and 36 percent of low-wage employees and blue-collar workers, respectively.[4] The demand for openness and/or protection is likewise marked by a pronounced social cleavage. The large metropolitan areas where the wealthier members of society live and work are more fully integrated with the world economy than smaller cities are; logically enough, it is here that executives in business and the liberal professions fabricate and disseminate the gospel of the open society. But this is no more than window dressing, a way of masking the relentless operation of modern commerce. Globalization—and the reign of a new kind of royalty, the market itself—does indeed represent an opportunity for the upper strata of French society. It promises them well-paid jobs and therefore the money needed to acquire ownership of property that formerly belonged to the working classes. The pretense of an open society makes it possible to present it in favorable contrast to a closed society that has withdrawn into itself, and in this way to diagnose the losers from globalization as embittered people who find it difficult to get along with others. The social question, of the seizure of jobs and wealth by the upper classes, is thus discreetly swept under the rug. Long live the law of the market.

Money

The upper classes love city life, trade, people unlike themselves. But if they congregate in the major urban centers, the main reason is money.

The dominant classes today profit directly or indirectly from a new economic and financial order. Not one industry of the major centers, from finance to broadcasting, has escaped control by the financial sector. Though members of the new bourgeoisie are opposed—completely opposed!—to big finance and globalization, they are all too pleased to share among themselves the fruits of a globalized economic model that rests on either exploiting the working classes or excluding them or both. With boundless good cheer, *Homo festivus*[5] amasses money, builds up a legacy for his children on the backs of the working classes, and votes for the left.

While a majority of the working class is confronted with unemployment and economic insecurity, the corporate upper class grows richer by the year. Since 2008, low-level employees and workers have experienced a sharp decline in their income,[6] while at the same time executives have earned more on average despite an unfavorable economic environment. Unemployment and the lack of job security, which affect primarily the working class, increase in proportion to the rate of metropolization, which is to say the rate at which skilled, well-paying jobs become more concentrated in the major cities. In 2012, the average monthly income of individuals in the wealthiest socioeconomic categories (business executives and senior members of allied professions) ranged from €2,400 to €4,300; among middle management, from €2,000 (for factory foremen) to €2,250 (for civil service administrators). For working-class jobs, income ranged from €2,000 at the upper end (secretaries and administrative staff) to €1,340 (unskilled artisanal workers—more than three times less than those of the upper classes). The same scale of inequality is found among retirees, since executives have pensions almost three times higher than those of workers.

There are unemployed executives, of course, as well as academics and other white-collar professionals who are unsure of being able to hold on to their jobs. Not everything is rosy for the upper classes. But unlike members of the working class, they live comfortably: if they lose their job, they can count on finding another one; they live in pleasant neighborhoods without fear of crime; they can afford to go away on vacation and send their children to university. They face no real difficulties, in other words, in keeping up a bourgeois lifestyle. Because they live in the most dynamic cities, the majority of them are able to maintain or improve their social position.

Money—but Also the Spoils

The rise in urban real estate prices is a source of permanent anxiety for the few renters who are left. The new upper classes have hastened to claim for themselves, simply by letting the market work its magic, most of the supply of private housing that once was occupied by the less well-off. The process is conveniently obscured by a euphemizing semantics that renders the violence of class conflict invisible. Some fifteen years ago, while studying the renovation of working-class neighborhoods, which by the late 1990s was being undertaken on a large scale throughout the country, I sought to show that class conflict was knowingly being concealed by the use of the neutral term "gentrifier." It was in this connection that I borrowed the term "bobo," shortly after David Brooks's book first appeared.[7] It immediately provoked a backlash in the media and academia.[8] What infuriated my critics was that the expression "bourgeois bohemian" contains the word "bourgeois." It is typical of the new urban masters that they try to hide their true social status, to give the impression of belonging to a majority middle class like everyone else. On the pretext that the term "bobo" is not sufficiently "scientific," they argued strenuously in favor of retaining "gentrifier," a vaguer word, more "urban," less "divisive"—and thus to their own advantage as members of a dominant class.

Among the new bourgeoisie, the scramble for spoils is seen to be an act of benevolence, proof of a concern for the weakest members of society. It is characteristic of the new bourgeoisie that it dresses up its class strategies in a rhetoric of altruism (community involvement, scholarship support for indigent students, and so on)—often sincerely, it must be admitted. Displaying compassion for the disadvantaged is all the easier, however, as it is addressed primarily to working-class immigrants, in such a way that the class relation is short-circuited by a reverence for cultural differences that represent no threat to the social domination of the upper classes.

Over the past two decades, the rate of eviction of the working poor from private housing has accelerated, to the point that they are now all but invisible in the major cities. Their disappearance is nonetheless the engine of a process of gentrification that the newcomers all pretend to regret.[9]

Exit the natives, enter the yuppies. The natives? The word is bound to cause a shudder. Let me be clear. I am talking about people who were born and who used to live in these neighborhoods, with no reference to ethnicity. But it is not only working-class people of French origin who have been expelled; immigrant youth who were born there and whose families can no longer stay there have been dispossessed as well. The virtual disappearance of private housing for low-income persons and the rise in the price of land have now effectively consigned a majority of the French people to the periphery. The working class, though it still constitutes a majority of the population as a whole, has become a vanishing minority in the largest cities. Île-de-France is the outstanding case. The boundaries of this region, where real estate prices are 9 percent higher than in the rest of the country, coincide with those of the Paris metropolitan area (which is therefore the nation's sole metropolis/region), making Île-de-France the only region in France where the working class is not a majority.

Gentrification steadily gathered momentum since first emerging several decades ago. The rate at which the worst off were forced out (and eventually much of the old middle class as well) was not slowed by the construction of public housing, for the question of who will live where and in what numbers is settled by the requirements of the labor market. That was true in the past, when the cities were industrial centers, and workers and other people of modest means were able to find private housing. It is true today, when the labor market, oriented chiefly to sectors of the economy requiring a highly trained workforce, no longer has any need of the working poor, except in some of the building trades, the public works sector, and the restaurant industry. The present system of public housing for a minority of the metropolitan population is intended to respond to these needs.

With executives and other highly compensated persons at upper levels of management making up 43 percent of the Paris workforce in 2012, the gentrification of the capital is by now an accomplished fact.

Covering the whole of the Île-de-France region, the Paris metropolitan area is the leading example of a still more significant phenomenon that is now making itself felt throughout the country. By the 1990s, the working class was already a minority presence in Île-de-France. As the only region of the country where this class did not constitute a majority, nothing prevented the classic dynamic of gentrification from operating on a larger scale. It gained yet more strength during the following decade, with the result that today working-class neighborhoods in the city itself have shrunk almost to nothing, scattered enclaves of public housing occupied predominantly by more or less recent immigrants. This marginal native and immigrant working-class presence has nonetheless permitted the champions of metropolization to go on talking about an open and diverse urban environment, even when the dwindling supply of public housing in Paris and the other major cities has only accelerated the eviction of the less well-off. A closer look at the geographical distribution of economic and social inequality will show that the new metropolitan model favors not openness and diversity but segregation.

An Open City at €15,000 per Square Meter?

Talk of open cities, of regional egalitarianism, of an economy from which everyone profits is belied by the reality of a real estate market that every day excludes a bit more of a working class whose interests the government pretends to defend by announcing unrealizable objectives of "social diversity." Only twenty years ago, €2,480 per square meter was the going rate for property in Paris. Today it is more than €8,000, on average, and in the affluent districts in the western part of the city and in the center it reaches more than €15,000. Prices have risen in every arrondissement, even in the traditionally working-class districts to the east and the north; indeed, it is the neighborhoods that workers and low-wage employees used to call home that have registered the greatest increases. The purchase by wealthy buyers not only of older apartments but also of raw space in converted commercial and industrial buildings has led to a dramatic change in the socioeconomic profile of neighborhoods in the center of the city and sustained an ongoing process of gentrification in the formerly working-class arrondissements to the east and the north, which have seen the price per square meter multiplied by as much as a factor of five.[10] Assuming that a worker could save €100 per month, it would take him or her the better part of a century to pay for one hundred square meters (a little more than one thousand square feet) at an average price of €10,000 per square meter in the old neighborhoods of Paris. If average prices are lower in Lyon, Toulouse, and Rennes, the upward trend everywhere has the effect of denying the working class of the surrounding region the opportunity to live in its major city.

An analysis of prices per square meter for France as a whole shows the major cities for what they are—new citadels that are inaccessible to the majority of the nation's people. To slightly modify the example I just gave, at an average rate of €10,000 per square meter it would take a French worker saving €100 a month (quite a lot for the ordinary wage-earner) more than eight years to buy a square meter of residential space in the capital—a little more than ten square feet, barely enough to sit down in! The marginal rate of increase in property values is still greater elsewhere. In London, for example, prime property can go for as much as €80,000 per square meter. Prices on this order mean that we are not talking about open cities but about closed cities, completely cordoned off. Contrary to what the official objective of social diversity is meant to suggest, there is no turning back. So-called gentrifiers typically acquire assets for themselves thanks to someone dying or putting a building up for sale. Members of the native working class today simply can no longer afford to live in strategically located areas. Public housing in outlying communities is now a last resort for workers hoping to be able to go on living near the major cities. These projects, mostly occupied by immigrant renters, are avoided by white French-born workers. Barring some utterly unforeseeable turn of events, their expulsion from the largest urban centers will be irreversible. The construction of 20 or even 30 percent more public housing blocks would not change the situation in any fundamental way. The new bourgeoisie has won. There is no dark intent to drive out the poor, no nefarious plot, only the implacable judgment of the market—in this case the real estate market, which accommodates as many or as few workers of various kinds as the labor market requires. What globalized cities need is a pool of trained personnel from the upper classes and the freedom, at the margin, to exploit unskilled immigrant labor. It's as simple as that.

This Is Our Home!

In their determination to distance themselves from the traditional bourgeoisie, members of the new bourgeoisie have embraced a déclassé lifestyle, stylishly slumming it in formerly working-class neighborhoods and hanging out in bars and restaurants that still retain something of their old proletarian atmosphere. This urge to identify themselves with the "people" depends on not actually having to deal with them. By recycling working-class culture, and disinfecting it in the process, they make it their own new and improved brand. Soccer is a perfect illustration. A sport that not so very long ago was an object of scorn and derision has now become the preferred entertainment of the new moneyed classes. Until France's triumph in the 1998 World Cup, soccer was generally looked down on by old money as a boorish amusement, a pastime for drunken proles. Suddenly the stadiums of the major cities (in France and throughout Europe) became vast outdoor tearooms: ticket prices soared, and soon the stands were filled by people with better manners and deeper pockets. On 6 February 2016, thousands of Liverpool fans staged a walkout at Anfield to protest prices of as much as £77 (the equivalent of €100).[11] In Paris, the Parc des Princes was deserted by supporters of visiting teams who were appalled by the amount of money asked for a match-day ticket. So long as the demand for seats continues to grow, especially in England, ticket prices will keep on rising. As in the old working-class neighborhoods of the major cities, what we are really witnessing is the replacement of one audience by another. In globalized cities, soccer has become the bourgeoisie's spectacle of choice. There are still a few working-class stands left in French stadiums, but not for much longer. In Paris, Lyon, and Lille, a new fan base chants the traditional war cry—"On est chez nous!" (This is our place!)—now that the working class has been driven out, not only from their old stomping grounds but from their old homes; too vulgar, too violent, too passionately attached to a city or a region or a country, there is nowhere in a gentrified and delocalized world for them to fit in. The English, who invented soccer, were the first to experience this change. The working classes disappeared from the terraces of the premier British soccer clubs. Working-class sporting culture lived on, only now far from the major cities, in the second- or third-division clubs of the medium-sized and small cities and rural areas of peripheral Great Britain.

Cohabitation and the Birth of a New Bourgeois Spirit

"We must stop kidding ourselves," the radical European parliamentarian Daniel Cohn-Bendit recently urged people of the left. "The UMPS does indeed exist."[12] In this case at least his meaning could not have been more clear: the two main parties of the center right and center left, the Union for a Popular Movement (UMP) and the Socialist Party (PS), might as well be a single party (UMPS); whatever differences there may be between them, they are minor compared to their common support for the idea of a France that is open to the world and international competition. Cohn-Bendit might also have added that these parties, like the others, are the product of a particular sociology, the society of globalization's winners, and of a particular geography, the France of the major cities. The hyperconcentration of the upper classes, in other words, has brought about a de facto cohabitation between the dominant elements of the right and the left. If they differ with regard to social questions, they agree on the thing that really matters: a globalized economy. The major cities are the consequence of a single-minded policy and portend the emergence of a single-party state.

A new bourgeois spirit animates the great urban centers today, the places where a majority of the upper classes live and work and manufacture a uniform way of talking and thinking about France's future and where today's dominant liberal-libertarian ideology first blossomed.[13] It was exactly this alliance, of individualism and the market, that opened the way to the present inegalitarian system. As the French left-wing *souverainist* Jean-Pierre Chevènement foresaw, nothing would remain of the traditional right or the left if the one abandoned the nation and the other abandoned society. Chevènement's nightmare came to pass, from the top down. Apart from a few inessential details, the upper classes on both the right and the left promoted the same view of the world. Two prominent mayors, the conservative Alain Juppé in Bordeaux and the leftist Gérard Collomb in Lyon, both supporters of globalization, deregulation, and multiculturalism, were for two decades the most visible faces of a common economic and social program.

This liberal/libertarian ideology perfectly illustrates a phenomenon that the historian Christopher Lasch was the first to perceive more than twenty years ago, namely, the betrayal of the people by the elites.[14] The metropolitan upper classes are the incarnation of what Lasch had earlier called a "culture of narcissism," itself the product of a "cult of the self,"[15] in which the community no longer exists—and not least because in the large cities the working class has all but disappeared. Liberated from the burden of taking an interest in the plight of the poor and the less well-off, the new urban egoists became ardent proponents of a globalized liberal order that strengthened their class position. Here again, the alliance of economic liberalism and cultural liberalism, which is at the heart of the phenomenon of metropolization encouraged by both bourgeoisies, shapes the ideological orientation of the governing parties. The invisibility of the working classes also made it possible to further concentrate wealth and jobs in the major cities and to justify weakening the protections of the welfare state. A few familiar figures from the latest edition of official statistics will give some idea of where things stand at the present moment: 6.1 million persons registered with the Pôle Emploi, a government agency helping the unemployed to find jobs and providing them with financial assistance;[16] 8.5 million living below the poverty line (defined as 60 percent of median income), or about 13 percent of the total population; 6 million earning the minimum wage; 3.9 million qualifying for assistance under the food aid program; 2.3 million eligible for minimum income payments; 3.8 million living in substandard housing;[17] 900,000 without a home of their own; 150,000 homeless.

As the chief beneficiaries of an economic and territorial system that also ensures their political and cultural hegemony, the upper metropolitan classes are the guardians of the neoliberal temple. They cannot be expected to challenge the dogma of globalization, of growth without jobs (for the least well-off), or of the international division of labor. It matters little that, for the first time in the nation's history, the working classes do not live where jobs and wealth are created. They live now in a peripheral France where daily existence becomes more difficult by the day.

A Neoliberalism That Welcomes
Public Subsidies for the Wealthy

Unwavering in its support for open markets, free trade, and the necessity of limiting income redistribution on behalf of the lower classes, the new metropolitan bourgeoisie nonetheless does not repudiate public subventions and redistributive social policies when they serve its own interests. The geographer Gérard-François Dumont has shown how dearly the major cities cost the nation through government subsidies, publicly financed facilities, and overrepresentation in regional administration councils, to say nothing of the virtually permanent urban-renewal projects in the suburbs of the major cities.[18] The degree of attention shown the banlieues, which has never been objected to by national or regional governments, regardless of the political tendency of their policies, is often cited as evidence of the altruism of the upper classes—a helping hand held out to disadvantaged minorities. The reality is less magnanimous. The metropolitan model is extremely inegalitarian, as we have seen. It rests on a two-tier labor market, with highly trained members of the upper classes on one level and immigrant workers filling unskilled jobs in the construction industry and service sector on the other.

It is therefore necessary to construct and maintain islands of public housing in metropolitan areas where a secondary class of labor can be housed. The poor districts on the outskirts of the major cities serve just this purpose. The problem is that, owing to the dual dynamic of gentrification and immigration, social, spatial, and cultural inequalities have continued to widen; and as a consequence of urban sprawl, these "neighborhoods" are now situated within the ambit of the country's wealthiest municipalities, the new medieval strongholds. This is apt to be an explosive situation, as suburban riots outside Paris in the fall of 2005 showed.[19] The apparent concern of the dominant classes for minorities and the banlieues masks a determination to exert control over populations that are useful to the local economy.

Government housing policy in the major metropolitan areas no longer has anything to do with altruism. If the share of public housing in the Paris region rose from 13.4 percent in 2001 to 17.6 percent in 2012, it was not for the purpose of creating the conditions under which the working class might return to live in the city itself but in order to keep an adequate supply of so-called key workers nearby.[20] These workers include medical personnel, teachers, police officers, and firefighters, many of whom no longer can afford private housing. Although municipal authorities are not bothered by the disappearance of the traditional working class, the prospect of losing the little people who ensure the continuity of public services is very much a cause for concern. Whether it is a matter of putting up immigrant labor in the lowest-cost public housing of the banlieues or key workers in the midrange public housing of the urban core, the free-market bourgeoisie is happy to support state investment when its interests are at stake.

This does not prevent the dominant classes from reminding their less fortunate fellow citizens how much they benefit from national solidarity, which would not be possible without disproportionate taxation of the wealthy. This way of talking, typical of both conservatives and socialists, which suggests that the upper classes, out of an obligation to serve the greater good, are a cash cow for the undeserving lower classes, is applied also to the forgotten expanse between the major cities: the peripheral France of the countryside, of the small and medium-sized cities, survives only thanks to the generosity of the great metropolitan areas, notably Île-de-France. On one side there are the prosperous urban centers whose residents are industrious and hardworking, on the other an impoverished land occupied by idlers and layabouts living on government handouts. This condescending attitude toward the working poor has been, for all intents and purposes, the attitude of the traditional bourgeoisie since at least the time of the Second French Empire in the nineteenth century.

Self-Segregation in the Service of Diversity

The metropolitan ideology rests in large measure on the myth of an open society in which everything is possible. As in Silicon Valley, ideas, perseverance, and a good computer will permit everyone to climb the social ladder.

The modern metropolis is imagined to be a field of dreams— dreams that can come true. Indeed, the lovely term *idéopôle* has been coined to suggest that, unlike the traditional *métropole*, it is in no way an emanation of old-fashioned capitalism.[21] Whereas metropolitan France is an incubator of new ideas and products, peripheral France is an intellectual void filled by people who produce nothing of real value. It is not surprising that the Silicon Valley model should be a point of reference for urban innovators in France. The US template is based on a liberal-libertarian ideology that "for decades has constituted the most perfect synthesis of the greed of free-market businessmen and the 'Californian' counterculture of the extreme left of the sixties."[22] One always neglects to mention that the richest people in Silicon Valley, from Bill Gates to Mark Zuckerberg, did not come from poor families; the "geniuses" of information technology all grew up in comfortable circumstances. In every respect the new world resembles the old one. From San Francisco to Paris, the new upper classes that promote the ideal of an open society practice self-segregation and the time-honored techniques of bourgeois co-optation.

Confidently huddled behind walls of money, these classes minimize their risks by residing in exactly those areas that are most lavishly provided with the highest paying private- and public-sector jobs. If they continue to uphold meritocratic ideals in economic life and government, they understand that maintaining their class position and assuring their children's success is guaranteed not by the virtues of the market, and still less by those of the Republic, but by isolating themselves from the rest of society. The effectiveness of this strategy should not be underestimated. It allows the new bourgeoisie to avoid appearing predatory; by appearing instead to be welcoming and charitable its members are able to do away with class conflict and silently reinforce their social position while passing along its benefits to their offspring.

Sons and Daughters of the Dominant Classes: The New Inheritors

It was an eternity ago, in 1964, that the sociologists Pierre Bourdieu and Jean-Claude Passeron documented the importance of family background, socially and culturally, in improving a person's chances of educational and professional achievement.[23] Since then everything has changed, for the worse. France's elite *grandes écoles* recruit more than ever from well-to-do families; discreet self-promotion and adroit networking do the rest, paving the way for success after graduation in the private sector. The sons and daughters of privilege are like fish in the water of this neoliberal society, where everyone-for-himself is the norm and republican meritocracy is a thing of the past. According to the Organization for Economic Cooperation and Development (OECD), in no country today does family environment have a greater influence on educational performance than in France.[24] Note, too, that this tendency is strengthened in proportion to the rate of metropolization.

The concentration of universities in major cities is evidently not new. After several decades of gentrification, however, the best ones are now centrally located in the most affluent regions. Access to higher education under these circumstances becomes difficult, if not impossible, for a young person from a working-class background in peripheral France. The new social geography carries on an already venerable process of social homogenization, particularly in the grandes écoles. By now the effects are so visible that some universities, such as the Paris Institute of Political Studies (Sciences Po), practice a form of positive discrimination by recruiting from the banlieues. Obviously this sort of targeted advertising in no way addresses the more general problem of putting higher education within the reach of students from poor families, particularly in outlying regions. For the majority of them, their educational experience will end at the age of eighteen with the *baccalauréat* examination (known informally as the *bac*) or, in the best case, with a technical course of study after high school in a vocational program. One recent report notes that "children of senior executives make up more than half of the students in the most selective schools (engineering, for example), whereas their parents represent only fifteen percent of jobholders. Conversely, the children of workers are better represented in short-term vocational programs [typically two years of study with an emphasis on technology in a specific field], in addition to schools training paramedics and social workers."[25] At the master's and doctoral level, children of workers and other low-wage employees account for 17 percent and 12 percent of all degree candidates, respectively (whereas their parents make up 52 percent of the labor force). Furthermore, access to higher education for children of the working class has been unchanged, or actually has become more restricted, since 1990. In the grandes écoles, the bourgeoisie has taken up permanent residence, with sons and now daughters following their fathers at the École Polytechnique, the Hautes études commerciales (HEC) school of management, and Sciences Po. In these and other top schools, diversity stops at gender parity and geographic distribution. A study of the prestigious Institut national des études territoriales (INET), which trains candidates for positions in regional public administration, shows that women are well represented there, on a par with men, and that graduates come from every region of metropolitan France and its overseas departments. The problem is that both the men and the women come from the same social backgrounds: the fathers of more than 60 percent of the students are executives or retired executives (whereas working-class students account for only 8 percent of the graduates).[26] Future regional administrators may therefore be counted on to spread the ideology of the dominant classes and impose a single model of development, metropolization, in every corner of the land. The majority of students from the working class, when they do manage to continue their studies beyond the bac, earn worthless diplomas from unimportant universities. The time of republican meritocracy may be past, but it has not been replaced by an economic meritocracy.

Economic and social recomposition on a regional level puts the finishing touches to the system of social reproduction identified by Bourdieu and Passeron. From start-ups to large companies, from journalism and the other media (including cinema) to finance, the most highly skilled and best paid positions are disproportionately located in the large cities. This concentration (61 percent of executive positions in 2010 were located in metropolitan areas of more than five hundred thousand inhabitants, with the Paris region by itself representing 35 percent of the total) favors the gentrification of these places and self-segregation—which is to say the social reproduction of elites. Paradoxically, then, globalization has had the effect of undermining the old meritocratic assumptions of business and public administration. In contradiction to the liberal ideals they celebrate, the new upper classes have placed their faith in nepotism (with the understanding that the "son of so-and-so" will be followed in due course by the "grandson of so-and-so"). This is true not only in the private sector but also in the ranks of the senior civil service, which recruits almost exclusively from the bourgeoisie.

The Silicon Valley model of open capitalism is unlikely to alter this state of affairs in any significant way: most start-ups in France are the creation of inheritors. The journalist Jean-Laurent Cassely points out that 83 percent of these start-ups were founded (or cofounded) by graduates of a grande école (with a bachelor's or an advanced degree), 16 percent by graduates of a less prestigious university (French or foreign), and only 1 percent by persons without a university education.[27] The transparency promoted by a company such as NUMA, a Paris-based digital innovation hub whose mission is to accelerate private tech-based business development, has exposed the current degree of homogeneity in this sector to public view. According to a study on start-ups in their early phases, recently published by the global business consultancy Roland Berger, the founder typically is a man (81 percent), young (twenty-five to thirty-four in 60 percent of the cases surveyed), and a graduate of a leading business or engineering school (23 percent for each type of program, or almost half in total). A diploma from a grande école in one of these fields, earned by only 3 percent of the student population, has become the norm in digital entrepreneurship. Whereas the children of executives in business and other white-collar occupations make up half of the enrollment in the most selective programs preparing students for admission to the grandes écoles, they represent only about 15 percent of all students.[28]

Metropolization, through the patterns of self-segregation it mechanically produces, raises the system of inheritance described by Bourdieu and Passeron to its highest point. The open society of the major cities will soon coincide with the regional geography of social reproduction, and everywhere the spoils will be shared by the sons and daughters of privilege. This amounts to nothing less than an authorized confiscation of the benefits of globalization by a "cool" bourgeoisie that nonetheless proclaims its commitment to diversity. Conveniently, the random success of a small number of young people from the banlieues will make it possible to disguise the process of social reproduction taking place in the new citadels.

What does "diversity" really mean under these circumstances? The upper classes of the major cities, champions of the open society, claim to be devoted to improving the condition of minorities. If business is the meritocratic milieu they say it is, one should think that minority promotion would be common. Wrong, once again. The digital entrepreneur Paulin Dementhon,[29] the product of a background he describes as comfortable, though not wealthy, as the son of a business executive and a small-business owner, observes that "since the Internet and start-ups got big, a great many firms have been created and most of them by white men who went to HEC." Speaking of the inheritance of family businesses, Yvon Gattaz (former president of the country's largest employer federation, Mouvement des entreprises de France [MEDEF], and father of the organization's current president) remarked that "owners fall into one of two categories: those who believe that genius is hereditary and those who have no children."[30] Self-segregation and social reproduction are very largely responsible for aggravating a potentially volatile source of division among the young people of the major cities, between those who are from wealthy and/or well-connected families, most of them white, on the one hand, and those who are from poor immigrant families and who are tired of being lectured to about openness by people who advocate diversity while doing their best to protect themselves from it, on the other.

This situation is still more pronounced in the worlds of politics, the press, culture, and cinema, key sectors over which the dominant classes are careful to perpetuate their control.

Diversity in Politics, the Press, Culture, and Cinema

Let us not be too harsh. It is not simply because the supporters of diversity and openness have not migrated en masse to the banlieues of the major cities (though these monuments to public housing are not far away), or because they have not sent their children to the underperforming schools that minority children are forced to attend, that we should conclude that these believers do not practice the faith they profess. Where one chooses to live and raise children is not a trifling matter. Nevertheless one should think that people committed to improving the lot of the disadvantaged would choose to work in settings that welcome minorities. Let's take a closer look.

The Socialist Party, though it no longer actively defends the interests of the working classes (at least not since its turn to the right in 1983), remains a foremost advocate of diversity. It seems reasonable, then, to expect this party itself to exhibit a high degree of cultural and ethnic diversity. And yet, as two national secretaries wrote in a recent op-ed piece in *Libération*, "thirty years after the March for Equality and [despite] years of militancy in the Socialist Party, one still has to hold a gun to the heads of party leaders in order to make progress."[31] The statistics marshaled by the authors are damning: 1 percent of metropolitan parliamentary deputies, 5 percent of regional council-lors, and only fourteen general councillors among the nation's ninety-six departmental councils come from a minority background; only one ambassador and three prefects, out of the fifty-two chosen by the chief of state, come from a minority background. The situation at the ministerial level is even less reassuring: of the 140 principal private secretaries or chiefs of staff and their assistants, only 5 have "non-European" names. And within the Socialist Party itself, out of 203 members of the National Council, only 7 are from minority back-grounds (in some departmental authorities, none at all).

Are diversity and antiracism therefore nothing more than slogans, a cynical attempt to sway minority voters? The short answer is yes. Like Sarkozy, who duped working-class whites by publicly taking a hard line on immigration while at the same time working behind the scenes to redirect the flow of foreigners into the country without re-ducing it,[32] the Socialist Party courted the votes of poor blacks and *beurs* (second-generation North Africans) by treating them as victims and branding all dissenting opinion on the subject as fascist. Rhetoric about diversity has never been seriously acted on; there has never been any corresponding willingness to create jobs for poor whites. The management of working-class neighborhoods for political purposes, as well as the unhopeful diagnosis of their condition given by experts close to the party, has always had a whiff of paternalism about it. Both the promotion of "participatory democracy," which is to say citizen involvement in political decision-making, and the woolly concept of "empowerment" in the neighborhoods are aimed only at winning votes and buying social peace—not at sharing any real power. Second-generation citizens, especially in the banlieues, understand this perfectly well.

Socialist leaders are not the only ones to call for a mixed and open society. Members of the press, many of them quite influential, have been no less disappointing in this regard. A majority of the profession supports the socialist left: in the first round of the 2012 presidential election, 39 percent of journalists said they had voted for François Hollande, 19 percent for Jean-Luc Mélenchon, and 18 percent for Nicolas Sarkozy (only 3 percent of those surveyed said they had voted for Marine Le Pen); in the second round, 74 percent chose Hollande.[33] This preference is likely to endure, since polls of journalism students gave 40 percent of the votes to Hollande and 25 percent to Mélenchon.[34] The regulatory agency responsible for monitoring electronic media practices, the Conseil supérieur de l'audiovisuel (CSA), recently deplored "the absence of diversity in the journalism sector."[35] Not only the editorial staff of the mainstream press but also the student body in leading schools of journalism remain hopelessly homogeneous, bourgeois and/or white—a situation that is apt to be intensified in the coming years as the mainstream press struggles to cope with competition from digital outlets, which cannot help but reinforce the natural tendency of the upper classes to self-segregation and co-optation.

The audiovisual field, including radio and television in addition to cinema, has long been united in applauding diversity. Once more, rhetoric is contradicted by reality. Notwithstanding the film industry's reputation as a pillar of the struggle against racism and on behalf of a mixed society, it is one of the most inbred sectors of the global economy. In March 2016, the Academy Awards ceremony in Los Angeles was the occasion of a bitter controversy over the absence of black actors from the list of nominees. The show's host, the black comedian

Chris Rock, began by humorously welcoming the audience to the "White People's Choice Awards" and went on, in the nicest possible way, to denounce Hollywood as a racist club. Rock put his finger on the essential point: the perverse ideology of a dominant class. Officially benevolent with respect to diversity and antiracist as a matter of principle, the US film industry is a self-segregated society that perpetuates a system of social reproduction in Bourdieu's sense. Just two days before the Oscars were handed out, the César Awards ceremony had taken place in Paris. France, everyone there would have agreed, is obviously more open to diversity than racist America is. The proof in this case was supposed to be that the jury gave the best picture award to the film *Fatima* (a story of the difficulties faced by an Algerian cleaning woman in raising her children), allowing the presenters to praise the virtues of diversity in front of a singularly white and well-heeled audience. Is the French situation really any different? Here again we have a monoracial industry that long ago mastered this routine, congratulating itself on making a film that features a Franco-Arab domestic servant in order to give the impression of open access to one of the most closed economic and cultural milieus in the country.

The phenomenon of self-segregation is not confined to cinema. It pervades the entire world of the arts and culture (which nonetheless misses no opportunity to hold forth on the subject of otherness), as a broad-based group called Décoloniser les arts, formed to denounce "the absence of diversity in the theater, in the plastic arts, and in French disciplines and cultural centers generally," has taken upon itself to point out.[36] As for the arts public, moviegoing remains still today by and large an upper-class recreation in France: in 2012, only 55 percent of workers went to the movies at least once a year, as against 82 percent of senior management; for the theater and museums, the respective percentages fall to 23 percent and 20 percent for workers, as against 63 percent and 69 percent for managers.[37]

Whenever someone asks what accounts for the low representation of minorities in the parties of the left, cultural institutions, and the press, responsibility is immediately assigned not to leading figures in these fields and organizations but to society as a whole. The fault lies with "racism," with "discrimination," with "public opinion," sometimes with a part of society, the "working class" (also known as "neo-reactionaries"), never with the sociocultural self-isolation of the upper classes. Nevertheless, it is a rather simple matter for white elected officials, producers, and editors in chief to promote diversity: one has only not to let one's job get in the way.

The Fig Leaf of Diversity

The promotion of diversity as part of a policy of openness is therefore merely a way of concealing the essential fact, namely, the nonrepresentation of the working class as a whole—white, black, Arab—in the places of economic, political, and cultural power. Poor whites are no more present than blacks or beurs in the National Assembly (workers and low-wage employees made up only 1.9 percent of parliamentary deputies in 2012, as against 20 percent in 1946) or in cultural institutions. The debate over ethnic minorities in the television industry likewise masks the fundamental question of the representation of the working class. It is telling that 57 percent of invited guests on French television programs occupy senior management positions; only 2 percent are workers. Persons without a formal occupation (children, students, homemakers, the unemployed), who make up 38 percent of the population, account for only 10 percent of those who appear on television; retired persons, 20 percent of the population, account for only 3 percent.[38]

Control of television and cinema production makes it possible to give the impression of a peaceable, integrated, and indeed well-off society by making the majority of the working classes invisible. Films, television series, documentaries—written and produced by the bourgeoisie and financed by multinational corporations and/or by public groups under political direction—are at the heart of cultural domination. Although the traditional press now has much less influence than before (fewer readers, fewer papers and news magazines), the major communications conglomerates still find it worth their while to hold an ownership stake in the most prominent titles. All newspapers today, without exception (whether on the left or the right), are the creatures of communications conglomerates, banks, arms manufacturers, luxury-goods producers—all of them global corporations needing to promote the benefits of an open society. Self-segregation in the worlds of media and culture is the condition of the system's survival. Hidden behind a rhetorical façade of openness, the upper class is able to perpetuate, and indeed to strengthen, its dominance in the name of diversity.

The No-Boundaries Advocates of Invisible Boundaries

Immigration, as we have seen, is concentrated mainly in the large cities. The change from a century ago, when workers typically came to France without their families, to the present tendency for entire families to leave their homelands together has accentuated a dynamic of urban settlement that has been at work for several decades now. The demographer Michèle Tribalat has recently shown that, since 1968, the share of young foreign-born people has strongly increased in metropolitan areas of more than one hundred thousand inhabitants, reaching a level of 35 percent in 2011, while remaining stable in towns of fewer than ten thousand inhabitants.[39] As a crucial element of the sociology of major urban centers, immigrants live near, though not actually among, the upper classes. Without the proximity of the banlieues, members of the new bourgeoisie would not be able to pride themselves on living in a diverse and open city.

But if the elites and their prosperous allies uphold the ideal of openness to the world and to others, at the same time they consolidate invisible boundaries that, by aggravating geographic and cultural inequalities, give rise to segregated metropolises. They wish to be close to the immigrant—but not too close.

The social and cultural homogenization of the banlieues is every bit as much the product of the real estate market as the upper classes' habit of residential avoidance. Not a day passes that politicians, journalists, and academics do not instruct their audiences in the importance of openness and the necessity of favoring social and ethnic diversity. And yet, despite the ambitious projects of urban renewal in underprivileged neighborhoods that have been inaugurated in pursuit of this objective,[40] little has changed.

No Bobos to Be Found in La Courneuve

Incredible though it may seem, for almost thirty years now the political class, led by the left and aided by the intelligentsia, has bemoaned the decline in diversity, the rise in xenophobia, and the overconcentration in the banlieues of poor immigrants who foment jihadism. For thirty years it has been telling us that what needs to be done, in order to remedy the educational underachievement of young people (particularly young people of North African and sub-Saharan extraction), is to get serious about integration by restoring social balance in the country's elementary and middle schools. And the result after all this time? Nothing.

In many parts of France, suburban communities welcomed the prospect of internal immigration by members of the wealthier and more educated classes. In La Cité des 4,000, a neighborhood of La Courneuve outside Paris (the name refers to the number of new housing units built there in the 1960s), in Reynerie and Bellefontaine near Toulouse, in Lille-Sud, in Les Minguettes (Lyon), and in Monclar (south of Avignon, perfectly situated for patrons of the arts festival held there every year), mayors and city councils were prepared to make available blocks of attractive residences in newly renovated neighborhoods (and, in one case, a northern district of Marseille, apartments with a view of the Mediterranean).

Bizarrely, unless official statistics are somehow in error, no large-scale relocation to these banlieues has been recorded during the intervening decades. The exhortations of all those who advocate "deghettoization" and living together in harmony seem to have gone unheard. Even though these neighborhoods are not far outside the cities in question (La Courneuve is ten minutes by rapid transit from the center of Paris), even though they are well equipped with educational and recreational facilities, they did not manage to attract the very people who were convinced of the urgent necessity of reintegrating poor communities into the mainstream of the nation's social life. For the sociologist and urbanist Christine Lelévrier, one of the leading experts on public housing and patterns of residential segregation in France, the facts speak for themselves: after more than ten years of urban renewal, there has been no significant relocation of wealthier families to working-class neighborhoods, no significant degree of gentrification; to the contrary, urban renewal has led to a "reconcentration of socially homogeneous populations on the scale of [both] neighborhoods and buildings."[41]

As in US cities, when executives and senior members of the academic and liberal professions change their place of residence, they almost always move to bourgeois neighborhoods or neighborhoods in the process of being gentrified, very seldom to neighborhoods in which local housing regulations prohibit property ownership, whether of formerly public units or of private apartments in need of renovation. In the major cities, in other words, whites move into white neighborhoods or neighborhoods being gentrified, where they may expect their investment to increase in value. In the unlikely event that they do "cohabit" with immigrant families, in so-called mixed neighborhoods, they typically erect invisible barriers to social intercourse: by living in financially exclusive buildings (the wall of money) and by finding alternatives to sending their children to local public schools. If they had not left their old all-white neighborhoods, the defenders of openness would not have had to avoid exactly the segregated school districts that they maintain must by all means be desegregated. Nowhere is the problem of steering clear of substandard elementary and middle schools (in which the majority of pupils are the children of sub-Saharan and North African immigrants) more challenging than in Paris itself. Bobos there have no intention whatsoever of putting the future of their own children at risk. Blithely ignoring their own multiculturalist blather, they will therefore send their children to selective public schools or, in the "worst" case, pay tuition at a private school. Diversity—real multiculturalism—is for other people.

The avoidance behavior of the upper classes, in response to the dual dynamic of gentrification and immigration, perceptibly reinforces patterns of segregation in all of the major cities. In Paris, despite its professed openness to minorities, despite very slight public opposition to immigration and correspondingly little support for the National Front, geographic segregation is increasingly pronounced. Although children of immigrants accounted for 20 percent of French youth in 2011, in the Paris region rates of 77 percent were registered in the suburbs of Aubervilliers and La Courneuve and almost 70 percent in Saint-Denis and Sarcelles—levels of concentration also observed in other metropolitan areas. In Vénissieux and Vaulx-en-Velin, outside Lyon, the proportion of immigrant youth (officially defined as persons having at least one parent who was born outside France) is about 57 percent.[42]

The Fantasy of Class Solidarity

In the gentrified neighborhoods of the major cities, the superficial display of solidarity with immigrants permits bobos to contemplate an idealized version of themselves as united with the lower-middle class and the working class. In fact, as we have seen, the social and cultural distance between them is daunting, even in mixed neighborhoods. The journalist Géraldine Smith recently recounted the experience of a white family that moved to a predominantly Islamic neighborhood in an eastern district of Paris, the eleventh arrondissment[43]—a rude awakening both for bobos who long for a "united and fraternal Republic"[44] and for Salafis whose way of life is the opposite of that of the upper classes. Here, as in all such gentrified and mixed neighborhoods in France, the cultural and social divide has never been bridged. There are no objective grounds for an alliance between the working class and the lower-middle class, quite simply because their economic interests and cultural preferences are very different. And yet talk about the benefits of multiculturalism is meant to encourage exactly this belief, that such an alliance is in fact possible. Where cohabitation does occur, however, we have seen that invisible boundaries reproduce the classic relations of social domination, subjecting servants—the cleaning woman, the nanny, the worker hired to renovate the apartment, the dishwasher in the restaurant down the street—to the will of their wealthy employers and patrons. The differential economic status of the people who live in mixed neighborhoods—renters of public housing, on the one hand, and owners or renters of private housing, on the other—reinforces this social distance. If an alliance between the working class and the lower-middle class is improbable, an alliance with the boboized upper classes is purely an illusion.

Who Will Look After the Nanny's Children?

"The arrival of refugees is an economic opportunity," Emmanuel Macron declared in 2015. "And too bad if [it] isn't popular."[45] This statement, by a future French president, neatly summarizes the cultural divide between the dominant upper classes and the working class. Understandably reluctant to join Macron in welcoming yet another wave of immigration, poor whites in the periphery now find their concerns swept aside. It has been little noticed that their grievance was strongly echoed in the banlieues, particularly among members of the established immigrant working class. The reason is clear enough: the inhabitants of public housing in these neighborhoods know that integration of the new arrivals—cohabitation at €1,000 per month, over a long period—will actually take place in the buildings and the schools of their neighborhoods, not in the bourgeois-bohemian neighborhoods of the city centers. For them there is no sharing of wealth, only of poverty.

But Macron says nothing about any of this. He is speaking the familiar language of employers and business owners. If the international division of labor[46] makes it possible to reduce wage costs by replacing European workers with Chinese and Indian workers, immigration allows industries and services that cannot be moved offshore to practice social dumping in another way. The need for cheap local labor is all the greater as the traditional working class no longer lives in large metropolitan areas. The demand for unskilled and low-skilled labor in the major cities is very largely met by immigrant workers, particularly in the construction industry, the restaurant business, and parts of the service sector. Immigration makes it possible not only to satisfy the market's needs for cheap labor but also to keep the total wage bill for nonunionized workers as low as possible. A system of this sort for exploiting cheap labor therefore depends on a continuing influx of immigrants. Moreover, if MEDEF, the country's largest employer federation, favors a continuing high rate of immigration, it is primarily for the purpose of instituting a regime of permanent competition, not between natives and immigrants but among immigrants themselves, precisely in order to prevent any rise in the total wage bill. This policy also serves the interests of the new urban bourgeoisie. It is not by chance that the view "there are not too many immigrants in France," in response to a recent poll on the question, is a majority opinion only among executives (54 percent, as against 38 percent for middle managers, 27 percent for workers, and 23 percent for low-wage employees).[47]

However often the partisans of the open society express an apparently unselfish willingness to welcome immigrants, their moral generosity is nonetheless not devoid of self-interest. Immigration permits people who are not wealthy in the usual sense to enjoy a very comfortable standard of living in the most expensive cities of France. The low wage paid to the Malian immigrant working in a restaurant kitchen, for example, allows bobos to pay fifteen euros for lunch rather than thirty. In much the same way, if the new winners from globalization cannot afford "domestic staff," as the traditional bourgeoisie was able to do, the services of an immigrant cleaning woman or nanny are nonetheless well within their means (and all the more as these services may entitle employers to a tax break if they are formally declared, something that obviously is not always the case).

Nor is today's bourgeoisie any less disingenuous than yesterday's. It insists on the need to emancipate the poor and help immigrants, but its own lifestyle and standard of living are closely tied to keeping these same people in their place, both in France and abroad. This process is conveniently obscured by substituting a sanctimonious appeal to cultural differences for the unpleasant reality of class antagonism. The delicate question of who benefits from immigration is very seldom raised, the taboo subject of social and cultural domination never. When a bobo hires the services of an African nanny on the cheap, for example, what used to be condemned as exploitation of the proletariat is now praised as an exercise in intercultural understanding. But if she takes care of his children, who will take care of hers?

The Hashtag Left: Parable of a Closed World

Metropolization has built its new citadels. Protected by walls of money, the upper classes are now in a position to fully profit from the benefits of globalization, and this all the more as they have forgotten, in their splendid isolation from peripheral France, that a working class still exists—a fact that politicians, journalists, and television talking heads rarely mention, so careful are they to make their rhetoric conform to the views of the upper classes. A society that imagines itself to be open to the world turns out actually to be just the opposite. Sure of the rightness of their economic and social convictions and of their own moral superiority, the new urban overlords play a decisive role in shaping public perceptions, as well as the approved way of talking about society that accompanies them. Paradoxically, it was just when the upper classes achieved a hegemonic position, occupying by far the largest part of the political, academic, and media landscape, that they lost their legitimacy in the eyes of the working class, which is to say a majority of the population. The discourse of the elites no longer has any credibility; it is addressed to a France of privilege, a solipsistic world having no roots in reality, a sort of void. The social conscience of the urban centers, in its public expression, is a parable of a closed and empty world.

Gentrification in the major cities has very nearly made democratic freedom of expression an upper-class monopoly. The great public demonstrations, amply covered by the media, give voice almost exclusively to the opinions of the moneyed inhabitants of these cities. Just as the traditional bourgeoisie, people of the right on the whole, made up most of the crowds that marched in opposition to the idea of "marriage for everyone" in late 2012 and early 2013, so the new bourgeoisie, generally left leaning, contributed most of the people who took to the streets in support of *Charlie Hebdo* in the wake of the January 2015 terror attacks in Paris. The two cases have this in common: the virtually total absence of people from the working class (whether from the banlieues or from peripheral France) and the overwhelming presence of people from the metropolitan upper classes, almost by definition white and educated.

The gross underrepresentation of the working classes in social movements today is a direct result, of course, of the political disengagement of people who for many years now have felt that they are no longer represented by their elected officials, by unions, or by the media. But it also has to do with the disappearance of these same people from the major cities. For many of them it is difficult, as a practical matter, to participate in demonstrations that take place far from where they live. More fundamentally, however, the gentrification of public protest is proof of a corresponding disconnection of the upper classes from the rest of society, not only members of the working class in peripheral France but also in the banlieues, who are fully aware that the rebellocracy has not spoken for the less well-off for a long time. The failure to enlist the support of the most vulnerable members of society (the poor and chronically unemployed, undocumented immigrants, and so on), the unrepresentativeness of the unions (fewer than 5 percent of union members work in the private sector), and the co-optation of popular demonstrations by the most secure members of society show that social protest movements no longer address the concerns of a majority of the country's population.

Dissent now takes the form of a managed and convivial display of dominant opinion, a sign that we are living in an age of "supervised struggle" in which street demonstrations have come to acquire a festive character.[48] One variant of the new style of bourgeois mobilization, colloquially known as slacktivism, is a lackadaisical way of showing support for a cause that falsely gives the impression of actually engaging in meaningful social protest. Perhaps the most prominent example of this type, clicktivism, involves the use of social media to organize petitions expressing opposition to government policies or corporate practices. In February 2016, it gave rise to an unprecedented campaign through online social networks against a proposed reform bill brought before Parliament by Myriam El Khomri, the labor minister, that would make it easier for companies to lay off workers, cut down on overtime, and reduce severance payments. As the journalist and author Jean-Laurent Cassely has remarked, this sort of armchair activism seldom requires participants to commit themselves to anything more than a click and a like on Facebook and rarely has any practical consequence.[49] But it does attract the attention of the mainstream media.

Unsurprisingly, the new breed of activists comes mostly from the most gentrified metropolises. A study made by the newspaper *Le Parisien* on the basis of the postal codes that petitioners supplied to the website Change.org revealed that they were concentrated in seven major cities: Rennes, Nantes, Bordeaux, Toulouse, Montpellier, Grenoble, and, of course, Paris (especially the most highly boboized arrondissements in the eastern part of the city).[50] This geography coincides with the bastions of the left and the upper classes. Conversely, the regions and departments of peripheral France that are most affected by unemployment and underemployment (notably among them Marne, Ardennes, and Pas-de-Calais) were indifferent to grand attempts at cybermobilization. Having little sympathy for the hashtag left (#jesuisenterrasse, #nuitdebout, and so on),[51] the working classes remain aloof—even when, as in the case of the El Khomri law, they too are opposed to the government's policy. The uninvolvement of the working class is not due to any lack of interest in "politics" or "social questions." It is a result of the fact that the entire system of social and political representation is under the direction of the upper classes. Nor is the marginalization of the lower classes due to any deliberate policy of control from above. It is a consequence of the gradual gentrification of social struggles, formerly waged by an alliance of the lower-middle class and the working class and carried on today by populations that, having in the meantime become integrated, economically and/or culturally, enjoy a certain measure of comfort. It makes perfect sense that white-collar employees in the major cities who have achieved job security should want to defend a social status and class position that the working class lost long ago.

The journalist François Ruffin,[52] an organizer of the Nuit Debout movement that arose in opposition to El Khomri's labor reforms, is under no illusion as to what needs to be done. "What Nuit Debout has to do," Ruffin frankly admitted, "is break out from self-segregation."[53] No one would disagree that successful political struggle depends on the combined efforts of different social classes. But for a movement that is essentially a loose alliance of students, white intellectuals, and educated professionals, the number of classes is rather limited. Recognizing that it is now all but impossible to mobilize members of the working class who live outside the major cities, Nuit Debout therefore appealed to the last working-class neighborhoods still present in these areas, the banlieues. But even there it did not succeed in getting a foothold. The immigrant working poor did not feel that their interests were represented by a movement they perceived as being bourgeois and white.

The goodwill of the leaders of a movement such as Nuit Debout, genuine though it is, runs up against a reality that the dominant classes have so far not fully appreciated: the cultural alienation of the working class of peripheral France and the banlieues. Intellectuals and journalists fail on the whole to understand that they no longer call the shots, that ordinary people pay no attention to fine speeches and feel-good demonstrations organized by the elites. As the historian Jacques Julliard rightly observes, no social movement has ever been able to achieve its aims without an alliance of the lower-middle class and the "people."[54] But the fact of the matter is that this condition can no longer be satisfied. Several decades of unbroken alternation between center-right and center-left parties, of mistrust, condescension, and paternalism toward the working class, have produced a decisive break. The two worlds have separated, and the people at the bottom no longer grant any legitimacy to attempts at mediation by politicians, union leaders, community organizers, or intellectuals. Why? The dominant classes have won support for their economic and territorial agenda not only from the whole of the media and academia but also from the metropolitan lower-middle class. Under the circumstances, it is hard to see how an alliance between the people and the lower-middle class could come about, much less make any lasting difference.

But if the dominant classes have little to fear from movements that emerge from the globalized metropolitan areas, they have every reason to dread the prospect of growing unrest among the working poor in the banlieues and in peripheral France. The *bonnets rouges* (red caps) movement, which appeared in Brittany in October 2013 in reaction against a new highway tax levied on exhaust emissions from truck transport and against layoff severance programs in the food-processing industry,[55] has attracted strong support from labor, elements of civil society, and political groups. It is a harbinger of the radicalization of rural areas and small towns that now begins to make itself felt throughout the land.

2

An Americanized Society

Ever since the national referendum to ratify the European Union in 1992,[1] the real divide has been between neoliberals and sovereignists, between the winners in the contest of globalization and the losers, between the great cities and peripheral France. This sociocultural split is not specific to France; with the steady adaptation to a global economic regime and the reaction of the working class against it, the same cleavage has appeared in all developed countries. Everywhere the system of open markets and free trade creates its own internal resistance. From peripheral America to peripheral England to peripheral France, dissent has grown in areas that are now home to a majority of people of modest means, people who used to belong to the middle class.

The social and cultural crisis of identity that affects the whole of the developed world today is a consequence of the hollowing out of the middle class in a majority of professional categories. Government policies have been powerless to stem the rising tide of globalization. France has become an American society like the others, an inegalitarian and multicultural society in which the middle class shrinks, social and geographical imbalances become more destabilizing, and a tense standoff between the classes takes the place of shared interests.

The global economy, which rests not only on an international division of labor but also on advances in mechanization (particularly the increasing use of industrial robots), no longer has any need of the relatively expensive and overprotected Western working classes. What it needs are low-cost workers in China, India, and Africa, together with executives (overpaid) and immigrants (underpaid) in the United States and Europe. The integration of economies on both sides of the Atlantic into a new world order has proceeded, in effect, by administering the largest scheduled layoff program in history. This massive and unprecedented eviction of the working classes was not announced, much less negotiated. It got under way in the early 1970s when the curves for gross domestic product (GDP) and unemployment became parallel. Since then, globalization has demonstrated its ruthless efficiency in discharging the low end of the labor force. In France, as elsewhere, the working class did not receive a formal notice of dismissal. Instead it was quietly relegated to places that from now on would be increasingly disconnected from the world economy. Nor was responsibility for this great transformation, which aligned France with the neoliberal norms of Anglo-Saxon societies, accepted by the political class. Instead it was reassigned to the implacable logic of free trade. Deferring to the invisible hand of the market allowed elected officials to adopt the pose of loyal republicans, devoted to the ideal of equality for all, while nonetheless signing one free-trade treaty after another and blamelessly acquiescing in the relinquishment of sovereignty. In France, as everywhere else, the havoc wrought by globalization assumed the form of an inegalitarian and multicultural society.

Jean-Pierre Chevènement was one of the first to perceive the impasse to which globalization was bound to lead, arguing fifteen years ago that a loss of sovereignty could not help but have grave economic and social consequences. Massive deindustrialization and growing job insecurity among the working class proved him right. But as a candidate in the 2002 presidential election, running under the banner of the short-lived Pôle Républicain, envisioned as a party for "republicans of the left and the right," the former interior minister received only 5.3 percent of the vote. The message was plain: the camp of equality and secularism had lost; worse still, it had not managed even to win the support of the working-class electorate whose fundamental interests it defended. Although Chevènement made a tactical mistake during the campaign in not raising the question of immigration (and the cultural resentment it generates among poor whites), it did not really matter. He had already lost the political and media battle. The campaign by the dominant classes to portray him as a fascist, led by his "old friend" Bernard-Henri Lévy, author of a well-known book accusing the French right of antisemitism,[2] who ceaselessly attacked sovereignism as "rubbish," proved to be remarkably effective. The old republican ramparts had been swept away, leaving the field open to globalism and Americanization. But how could it have been otherwise, faced with the combined onslaught of Wall Street, the CAC 40, and Hollywood?

In the years since, republican opposition to growing inegalitarianism has come more and more to seem like a bad movie. French politicians, even if they still talk like republicans, have based electoral strategy for some time now on a sectarian style of marketing perfected in the United States.[3] At the local level, elected officials no longer think twice about implementing nakedly divisive policies.[4]

The Forced Exodus of the Working Poor

"Real incomes for many low-wage workers in the West have only slightly increased over the past twenty-five years," the economist Branko Milanovic observes, "whereas those of the wealthiest have soared. In the mid-1970s, in the United States, the richest one percent of the population pocketed 8% of national income. Today the figure is roughly 20%." Inequalities have long been more pronounced in the United States, the heart of the global system. But they are becoming greater today in Europe, even in a country as traditionally egalitarian as Sweden. "The world economy," Milanovic notes, "rests on three independent factors that together reinforce inequalities: technological progress (which replaces people by machines manufactured in countries with low wage costs), deregulation, and growing competition from countries such as China and India."[5]

The forced retirement of the working class is not only a matter of making people unemployed; it also entails the marginalization, both geographically and culturally, of all those who no longer have a place in a global economic system. Over the past few decades France has witnessed the steady departure of most low-income members of the labor force from the middle class. From factory workers to small farmers to wage earners in the service sector, the programmed expulsion of these categories has now very largely been achieved.

Politicians, seconded by journalists and academic experts, describe this layoff scheme as nothing more than an adaptation to new market conditions. They forget to add that these conditions are the product of an economic system in which the working classes of the developed world have been priced out. In order to accomplish their purposes, the dominant elements must rely not only on a political class that is wholeheartedly committed to participating in the benefits of globalization but also on an unfailingly submissive media and cultural class that diligently supports the cause by presenting a picture of French society that is deeply misleading in several respects. The object of the exercise is to institute a new economic order, highly efficient and highly inegalitarian, without anyone noticing. The way to do this is to make the losers from globalization invisible.

The first falsification of the facts consists in treating economic crisis and the unemployment that follows from it as a general phenomenon, indiscriminately affecting all social classes, with the result that executives as well as clerical and other low-level employees—the higher France and the lower France—are seen to suffer the effects of globalization together. And yet if one thing has remained constant for the past forty years, it is that it is primarily and disproportionately the members of the working class—industrial and other manual workers, office staff and nonmanual workers in general, small farmers and agricultural laborers—whose lives are made less secure by a changing economy. Upward social mobility has always been the exception for poorer people, of course; those who are born at the bottom typically die at the bottom. But the situation has grown markedly worse since the 1980s, to the point that sociologists now speak of a social "down escalator."[6]

Once upon a time the working class was economically and socially—and therefore politically—integrated in the life of French society. Despite difficult working conditions and low wages, workers were an indispensable part of the economic system; what is more, they lived where they worked, in the great industrial cities of the nineteenth and twentieth centuries. Today their services are of little or no value. They have now been banished from the places that create jobs and wealth, at a more or less great remove from the major urban centers.

The statistical evidence is very clear: unemployment, underemployment,[7] and economic insecurity are the lot of the lower classes—newcomers to the labor force, experienced workers, and retirees alike—not of the upper classes. According to a recent report, "Senior and middle management are virtually at full employment, with rates of unemployment of 3.9% and 5.2% respectively."[8] Conversely, the rate of unemployment for unskilled workers is five times higher than that of executives and three times higher than that of white-collar employees.

Low wages, job insecurity, unemployment, and underemployment affect the working poor to a far greater degree than they affect other categories. The rate of unemployment among unskilled workers is almost four times that of executives; that of skilled workers and salaried employees is double. Underemployment is a familiar condition in the service sector, especially in big-box retail chains where part-time restrictions on working hours are common. Additionally, with falling median wages approaching the minimum wage, the working poor are apt to be particularly hard hit by sudden changes in economic circumstances: the slightest personal misfortune (unemployment, divorce, illness) brings increased financial distress and, in the worst case, can lead to destitution. This predicament is experienced as a permanent state of anxiety, against which the redistributive resources of the state (welfare, unemployment benefits, and so on) offer little protection and still less consolation. The level of personal savings gives further insight into the forced exodus of a majority of low earners from the middle class. More than half the members of the labor force in France are unable to save enough on a regular basis to make any meaningful difference in their lives. In 2015, 54 percent of the working population said that they could not save more than fifty euros per month (about forty dollars); for a quarter of them, the figure does not exceed ten euros (less than ten dollars).[9] In France today, in other words, those who are able to save constitute a minority. Saving is now a privilege of the well-off.

The vast severance program being administered at the expense of the working class has been met with relative indifference. It would not be possible without the tacit approval and support of a sizable part of the population, which for several decades now has managed to turn to its advantage many of the economic and social opportunities available to elites. The shift from an integrationist model to a divisive inegalitarian model could not have occurred as easily as it did if it had benefited only the rich or only the banks.

It is tempting to suppose, as the philosopher Patrick Savidan remarks, that "the rich govern and that, in our immense majority, we are more or less manipulated . . ., that a tiny minority forces us to support social and political tendencies that are detrimental to our own interests. . . . That is going too far. To observe that the preferences of the wealthiest converge with the interests served by public policy is one thing, but nonetheless it does not suffice to establish that we have a problem only with the elites, with the rich."[10] Savidan is quite right to reject the suggestion of conspiracy. It should be noted, moreover, that the (legitimate) criticism of the rich and the (obviously legitimate) criticism of bankers are perfectly consistent with an international media regime that is effectively controlled by these same financial institutions and sponsors (not to mention the films and television series produced by Hollywood about Wall Street and the financial oligarchy). Denouncing the rich and the expropriation of working-class wage income by owners of capital poses no more of a threat to the system than coming out in favor of peace rather than war does, or in favor of brotherhood rather than racism! Criticism of the increase in inequality is tolerated for the same reason.

Ninety-one percent of the French agree that differences in income are too great (along with 92 percent of Argentinians, 90 percent of Chinese, 73 percent of Swedes, and even 65 percent of Americans). Dissatisfaction with the inegalitarian model is therefore very widely shared. And yet so immense a majority is strangely incapable of reforming a system run by only the wealthiest 1 percent! Once again the reason is that, while the famous 1 percent do in fact have at their disposal unprecedented financial and economic power, they manage to hold on to this power only by virtue of the fact that they have the support of a significant share of all those who benefit from globalization. So long as nothing interferes with this state of affairs, the adaptation of society at the national and regional levels to the demands of a global economy will continue.

Territorial reforms have been carried out in France in the name of regional equality to deal with the problem of uneven development.[11] As in the United States, where half of the increase in GDP is due to the growth of metropolitan areas, the greater part of wealth creation in France takes place in these areas: between 2000 and 2010, 75 percent of this growth occurred in the fifteen largest areas (higher than the average figure calculated by the OCED).[12] Metropolitan areas now account for 55 percent of total wages and 50 percent of economic activity; the GDP for these areas is also 50 percent higher than in peripheral France.

Isolated from the global economic system and excluded from the most dynamic sectors of the national economy, the working class has silently decamped from the major cities. As in the United States, as everywhere in the developed world, social, economic, and cultural inequalities between the major urban centers and the working-class peripheries now become ever greater.

Metropolization and Territorial Inequalities

In every country, regions are organized around an urban center. From New York to Milan to Beijing, economic development emanates from the great cosmopolitan cities. Metropolization, the domestic corollary of globalization, has wholly established itself as an incontestable fact. In the United States, as in France, metropolitan areas account for the majority of jobs and the better part of economic growth. There is no point bemoaning the existence of these engines of prosperity; they are here to stay. What we need to do is look more closely at how prosperity is distributed, at a system that deepens social and geographic inequalities while sweeping aside a little more of the working class every day.

London is the quintessential example of the citadel city in an age of metropolization. It displays all the characteristics of the new urban model. By 2015 the average monthly rent for an apartment had risen to £2,580 (€3,500, or almost $4,100), more than the average monthly salary of £2,300 (€3,150, or less than $3,700). The working class has all but disappeared.[13] What is left is a polarized labor market, with well-paid jobs filled by highly qualified personnel, on the one hand, and, on the other, poorly paid jobs filled by immigrant workers who are eligible for only very limited social protections. The traditional working class and the old middle class in London, for their part, have shrunk dramatically. "Between 2001 and 2011," the demographer Michèle Tribalat notes, "the number of British whites there fell by more than 600,000, even though the [overall] number of Londoners increased by a million. In ten years, the white British population [in the capital] shrank by thirteen percent (45% in 2011 as against 58% in 2001)."[14] Here the phenomenon of "white flight," perceptible in all the global cities, heralds the emergence of a peripheral Britain in which the traditional working class is now largely concentrated.

The metropolization of France has not yet reached the heights of English inegalitarianism, but the same dynamic is at work. Even if the dizzying prices of London real estate remain unrivaled for the moment, the Paris metropolitan region comes close: a ground-floor "loft" of nine square meters (less than one hundred square feet) on the exclusive Île Saint-Louis was recently put on the market for €50,000 (about $58,500).[15] As in Great Britain and the United States, social and cultural inequalities within the large cities continue to increase, and the geographic segregation of metropolitan areas from peripheral France becomes more and more noticeable.

Inequalities within Metropolitan Areas

The polarization of employment and the dual process of gentrification and immigration it sets in motion have the effect of reinforcing sociocultural inequalities within French metropolitan areas. The influx of immigrants, in particular, is channeled to neighborhoods with a large supply of deteriorating public housing and substandard private housing. Social tensions are higher in these troubled urban areas than elsewhere.

Louis Maurin, director of the Observatoire des inégalités in Tours, notes that "enormous differentials exist between underprivileged neighborhoods and the rest of the metropolitan areas in which they are located. The standard of living in these places is much below the average."[16] In 2014, average monthly household income in these neighborhoods—officially recognized as "sensitive urban zones"— topped out at €1,860 (about $2,175), as against €3,000 (about $3,500) in the rest of the surrounding metropolitan areas. The youngest inhabitants of these zones were on average three times poorer than children in neighboring communities.

Since 2008, inequalities have become greater. Between 2008 and 2012, the rate of unemployment in these zones rose from 16.7 percent to 24.2 percent, whereas in the other neighborhoods of metropolises containing such zones it rose from 7.6 percent to 9.1 percent: an increase of 7.5 percent by comparison with 1.5 percent. Between 2006 and 2011, the rate of poverty in the more than seven hundred sensitive urban zones in metropolitan France rose from 30.5 percent to 36.5 percent (an increase of 6 percent), whereas in the rest of France it rose from 11.9 percent to 12.7 percent (an increase of 0.8 percent).

This inegalitarian dynamic is at work in all the great cities—and nowhere more vigorously than in the Paris metropolitan area, which is coextensive with the Île-de-France region. A recent study on inequalities there noted that "while Île-de-France remains the wealthiest French region, the sociospatial contrasts are becoming more and more pronounced."[17] The analysis of income disparities shows that the communities of the inner suburbs are marked by growing segregation and polarization and that, although the incidence of poverty is now lower in the communities of the outer suburbs than it was, it has migrated across municipal boundaries. Between 2001 and 2011, according to a report published by the Institute for Urban Planning and Development (IAU), social polarization steadily gained strength in Île-de-France owing to an increase in average income in the municipalities nearest the urban core (the so-called chosen rim, freely selected by its inhabitants rather than forced on them by circumstances). Wealth is therefore increasingly concentrated in a belt of affluent communities, mainly to the west of the capital, although there are unmistakable signs of gentrification to the east as well. Considering the suburban public housing projects that are home to newer immigrants, the report emphasizes the role of avoidance strategies in helping to impoverish the banlieues, now largely "abandoned by native households," and notes that public housing is preponderantly occupied by sub-Saharan families that are "least advanced in the accumulation of household capital and [that] typically try to send money back home rather than save with a view to ownership."[18] The French geographer Christine Lelévrier has shown that urban redevelopment policy has done little to restructure patterns of socioeconomic distribution, in part because demolition of older housing stock has the effect of reconcentrating households, particularly the least economically secure ones, in a given neighborhood or district rather than dispersing them over a wider area.[19]

On the scale of the metropolitan area—in the case of Paris, of the region—one observes a corresponding polarization of the real estate market, which recorded increases in both ownership (12.3 percent) and the share of public housing (10.2 percent), along with a decline in the supply of private rental units (many of them converted to public housing or put up for sale to private buyers) in the first decade of this century. The metropolitan model, itself a product of the polarization of the labor market, has therefore strengthened both geographic patterns of segregation and social inequalities within regions. This situation is potentially all the more explosive in the largest cities today as the social and geographic divide coincides with ethnic and cultural cleavages.

Inequalities across Regions

We have seen that the concentration of highly skilled labor, talented senior management, and above-average incomes in the major cities, by contrast with the growing economic and social insecurity of the periphery, has accentuated the inequalities between the two Frances. If the impoverishment of rural areas is often acknowledged, the decline of commerce in the cities of peripheral France is less noticed. Yet the downtowns in many of them seem almost deserted; in some streets building after building has a "For Sale" sign posted in front.[20] This hollowing out affects small and medium-sized cities of fewer than one hundred thousand inhabitants, such as Guéret, Tarbes, Agen, Villefranche-de-Rouergue, Moulins, Niort, Albi, Béziers, Vierzon, and Calais. In Nevers it is estimated that almost 20 percent of commercial premises are empty.

There are many reasons for this trend, but two stand out: depopulation and, above all, competition from volume retailers on the outskirts of the city. The larger metropolitan areas have also taken away a sizable number of administrative jobs and, with them, the small local businesses they used to support. Civil servants in Béziers, for example, have gone off to Montpellier. One can scarcely walk around the downtowns of small and medium-sized cities without encountering empty shop windows and shuttered businesses. Cities that attract tourists or that still have an active industrial base have some room for maneuver, but for others the immediate future looks much less promising: the rate of commercial vacancies has risen annually for fifteen years now, reaching a high of 8.5 percent in 2014 for the three hundred largest cities in France.[21] Bringing city centers back to life is a priority almost everywhere today.

Cuts in government funding place both urban and rural communities in a particularly difficult position. Municipal and regional councils find themselves caught in a bind between increasing public demands and decreasing capital endowments. A recent government report on job prospects in the coming decade cautioned that "industrial areas stricken by international competition and productivity gains that have survived thanks to public financing and income redistribution may find themselves subject to tighter budget constraints than in the past."[22] This situation will be all the more challenging as the territorial reforms of the past several years have further marginalized these areas in relation to the wealthiest cities—and this at a moment when sharp rises in public expenditures cannot be offset by new sources of financing, straining social cohesiveness throughout the periphery.

The transfer of jobs to the major cities and the loss of businesses in working-class communities portend a widening of the social and cultural divide in the years ahead. The same report, forecasting the employment situation in 2022, indicates that existing trends are likely to become still more unfavorable, particularly in periods of economic crisis. Unsurprisingly, the largest metropolitan areas have proved more resilient than the rest of the country. Between 2006 and 2011, the increase in employment was 2.6 percent in the Paris region and 4.7 percent in the largest provincial urban centers, as against 0.8 percent in other major areas; medium-sized and small cities actually lost jobs. The report goes on to note that the largest areas benefit from an "employment composition effect" (owing to larger service sectors and more qualified workers) and from the presence of a disproportionately large number of executives. In Rennes, Nantes, Bordeaux, Toulouse, and Lyon, the workforce registered significant gains.[23]

The predominantly industrial areas of peripheral France, by contrast, especially in the northeast and the center, recorded a drop in employment (particularly industrial jobs). Since the crisis of 2008, even highly industrialized parts of the west have suffered job losses. In all parts of the country, areas located outside lesser metropolitan areas, typically rust-belt cities and/or agricultural towns with fewer than one hundred thousand inhabitants, have been struck by rising levels of unemployment.

More disturbingly still, the report frankly acknowledges that most of the jobs that will be at risk in the years to come are located in peripheral France, the land of small and medium-sized cities and mixed rural/industrial areas. The most vulnerable categories will be small farmers and manual workers (in the engineering sector, the textile and leather trades, and various process industries). Nevertheless local rates of job loss may depart from the national average depending on the quality and condition of production equipment, demographic trends, and government policies. One thinks particularly of areas experiencing demographic growth along the Atlantic coast and in the south, where an in-place economy supported mainly by tourism and retirees should make it possible to muddle through.[24] From now until 2022, regions in the west and the south, as well as the Alps, may be expected to attract people (both working and retired) and businesses (catering chiefly to tourism), and the Paris basin, Pas-de-Calais, Lorraine, Limousin, and Auvergne ought to see moderate population growth; in Champagne and Ardennes, however, population will probably decline.

Caregiving services for the sick and the elderly are another promising employment niche outside the major metropolitan areas. On balance, however, the social and geographic divide between the two Frances is likely to widen further, since industries with a strong potential for job creation from now until 2022 are underrepresented outside the largest cities. Worse still, this tendency will not be counteracted in the event that economic conditions improve, because once again growth will be concentrated mainly in the largest cities. A recent forecast by France Stratégie, an agency attached to the prime minister's office (formally known as the Commissariat-General for Strategy and Foresight), does not dissent from the gloomy outlook for the working-class periphery, warning that "urban centers of fewer than 100,000 inhabitants and areas outside these centers could see their economic slowdown grow worse in the years to come."[25]

Combating private-sector job loss is all the more difficult as government indebtedness at both the national and regional levels rules out the possibility of compensatory growth in the public sector. In many regions, especially in rural areas and small cities, the public sector is the largest employer. Peripheral France therefore has no choice but to rely more heavily on bank lending in order to maintain basic public services and facilities, particularly in the health-care sector.

It is clear that the concentration of employment in the major metropolitan areas has been at the expense of rural areas and small and medium-sized cities. The relative decline of job growth in peripheral France is made more intractable by the fact that a majority of the nation's unemployed, as well as a majority of the working class, live in exactly these areas.

A Guaranteed Minimum Income

Public-sector job creation used to make it possible to sustain a more or less constant level of economic activity in many parts of the periphery, particularly in small cities where government-sponsored employment accounts for most of the available jobs. Today, with fewer and fewer private-sector jobs, peripheral France is confronted with a shortfall in public financing. Unavoidably, then, the result of growing municipal indebtedness is a growing dependence on private lenders.

Globalization has therefore led to an impasse that the dominant classes will do their best to ignore. At the most, rising inequalities across regions will be addressed by policies of incremental redistribution and/or marginal adjustment—never through the development of a complementary (or, in the best case, an alternative) economic model that local elected officials in peripheral France might actually support.[26] For the moment it is as though it had already been decided that workers would henceforth be officially reclassified as chronic welfare recipients. Under the new inegalitarian regime, the upper classes profit from the wealth they create, while the lower classes consume to the fullest of their meager ability, then hold out their hand and end up losing whatever independence they once had.

In the meantime, bizarrely (or perhaps logically enough), the idea of a universal basic income has been revived in France (also in Finland and Switzerland). The appeal of such a scheme is that it would do away with poverty by assuring every person of a minimum income, regardless of his or her occupation or lack of one, while indirectly redirecting financial flows to some degree toward persons of modest means. Promoted as much by policy makers on the left as by neoliberals, it nonetheless does not amount to a departure from the global economic system, much less a rejection of it; to the contrary, it reinforces this very system.

Interest in a universal basic income reappears at a moment when the government has given up trying to integrate the worst off economically and culturally, in effect giving official approval to the permanent social and cultural demotion of the working class. One cannot help but recall Joan Robinson's mordant quip, that "the misery of being exploited by capitalists is nothing compared to the misery of not being exploited at all."[27] Although a guaranteed minimum income might be contemplated as a temporary substitute for a comprehensive treatment of the problem of poverty, it is not a lasting solution for the lower classes as a whole. What may seem at first sight to be proof of the benevolence of the upper classes in fact serves only to strengthen an inegalitarian regime in which the working poor no longer have any place at all.

The Death of the Republican Assimilationist Ideal

In France, as elsewhere, globalization has given birth to a multicultural society wracked by nativist anger and immigrant paranoia, by separatist impulses on both sides, geographic segregation, and increasingly frequent ethnic violence—in short, a perfectly ordinary

American society. Willful abandonment of sovereignty and unswerving support for immigration by big business have combined to bury the republican assimilationist ideal.[28] For the moment, at least, the law of 1905 providing for free compulsory schooling and a system of social protection continues to safeguard France against the worst excesses of class antagonism. Even so, there can be no doubt that the fragmentation of French society is already quite advanced. And while debate between multiculturalists and republicans is no less heated than it was twenty-five years ago, the main issues have been settled by the intervening course of events. However fervently politicians may proclaim their steadfast devotion to the republican model of secularism and egalitarianism, the reality is that it has been superseded by sectarian intolerance and widespread civic mistrust.

Multicultural grievances are now a familiar feature of French life. In May 2016, to take only one of a great many examples, the white French-born coach of the national soccer team, Didier Deschamps, was accused of racism for not selecting players of North African descent. Few people seriously believe that Deschamps left these players off the squad because of their ethnic identity, and the affair will no doubt be quickly forgotten; nonetheless it gives some idea of the extent of cultural tension in French society today. In a country in which athletes and artists of Maghrebian ancestry[29] can call a white coach (with a very French name) "racist" because he did not choose enough "Arabs" (and therefore because he chose too many "blacks" and "whites"), the time may finally have come to be done with the old republican fanfare, to mute the trumpets once and for all.[30] With the rise of sectarian animosity, amid increasingly strident assertions of ethnic identity, we are witnessing the emergence of exactly the sort of divided society that a global economic order would lead us to expect. The United States has long exerted a strong influence on the working-class imagination, particularly among the younger generation. Nevertheless the underlying tensions are perceptible among people of all class backgrounds, and, as in the United States itself, the least spark is enough to set off a round of impassioned protests, if not also violent confrontation. In the suburb of Montreuil, northeast of Paris, a rumor of pedophilia involving a black child in a local nursery school provoked a sharp exchange between a vocal part of the black community and town hall, which was suspected of protecting a white predator. A group of protesters immediately insisted on the racial motivation of the alleged assault and received the support of black media personalities.[31] Even though the matter was subsequently dropped by the vice squad, in a commune with particularly deep social, geographic, and cultural divisions, where a sizable poor black community lives alongside an enclave of white bourgeois bohemians, it was a potentially explosive moment.

Reference to ethnicity, religion, and culture has become commonplace among working-class youth, not only "minority" blacks, Muslims, and Jews in the banlieues but even more so young French whites in the periphery, who now by a sort of mirror effect increasingly point to their own racial, religious, and cultural heritage. Like it or not, this is the reality of France today. No one speaks any longer of a common national interest, only of allegiance to a community in which each person is obliged to bear a prescribed sectarian identity. Minority groups were the first to think in these terms, but the habit has now been aggressively taken up by all members of the working class, whatever their ethnic background or religion. It is not by accident that whites should have become white, as it were,[32] during a period of demographic instability, in which majorities may abruptly be converted into minorities (and vice versa).[33]

"Living together in harmony is a joke," the historian Jacques Julliard recently remarked, "and a bloody one at that."[34] For Julliard, what in France is called communitarianism—the juxtaposition in a particular area of communities that differ in respect of geographical origin, language, religion, culture, philosophy—has turned out to be an enormous calamity. This opinion is now largely shared among political elites in Europe, from the former British prime minister David Cameron[35] to the German chancellor Angela Merkel, who, five years before German business leaders prevailed on her to welcome a million immigrants in 2015, expressed the view that "multiculturalism is a failure."[36] "If the phenomenon were to persist, Europe would not survive," Julliard added. "Multicultural nations now face a brutal alternative, with no way out: integration or civil war. Only the universal version of humanism, inherited from Christianity, the Enlightenment, and the French Revolution, will help us escape this disaster."[37] The problem is that the global economic system, in which sectarian tensions are an inevitable consequence of the very multiculturalism it ruthlessly enforces, has already taken aim and eliminated its rival: the republican assimilationist ideal.[38]

The new order has succeeded in imposing its authority with a minimum of fuss. In hindsight, it is clear that the error was to believe one could have the economic benefits of globalization without its social disadvantages, epitomized by American society. That ruled out the republican model from the very start. The sincerity of a political class that ceaselessly affirms its attachment to the republican model while promoting a system that condemns it in advance may therefore be doubted. Our elected officials well know, or should know, that a globalized society is indissociable from an age of shifting demographic majorities and minorities. It is a society in which other people are doomed to remain strangers to us, locked away in separate, preassigned, and impenetrable identities.

It is plain, too, that the political class in France has been able to exploit this transformation for its own purposes without any great difficulty. As in the United States, the major parties were quick to adopt the techniques of ethnocultural marketing. Far from upholding republican values, they constantly and discreetly appeal to voters' ethnic pride, religious beliefs, and cultural backgrounds. The columnist and essayist Céline Pina, a former Socialist regional councillor in Île-de-France, has mercilessly exposed the shameless duplicity of politicians skilled at praising republican values while at the same time currying favor with local community representatives. She cites a recent example involving the municipalities of Stains, Aubervilliers, Bagnolet, and Bondy, all of which have significant Muslim populations that support Palestine in its struggle against Israel. In June 2016, Bondy officially announced that it would boycott Israeli products. In the view of Laurence Marchand-Taillade, president of the Observatoire de la laïcité du Val-d'Oise, a leading center for the study of secularism, "these initiatives are being undertaken with increasing frequency by mayors of Paris's inner suburbs trying to attract Muslim votes. They betray a kind of contempt for the Muslim population, assuming that it can be bought, because it is supposed to be monolithically committed to the Palestinian cause."[39] Pina takes a still harder line, charging the political class as a whole with a failure to live up to its responsibilities: "We have entered into an era of inheritors without memory or political principles, of people who no longer have anything to defend if it does not advance their careers. Only the dregs are left, on the right no less than the left. . . . Elected officials [today] are second-rate. It is the end of a political generation."[40]

But the mediocrity of the political class does not suffice to explain the growth of sectarianism and, more particularly, of Islamism. These tendencies are also encouraged by the adaptation of Western societies to the new norms of a global economy. The weakening of the republican tradition has given cultural and religious groups on all sides unprecedented power. Owing to the sheer size of the Muslim population in France (estimated by Michèle Tribalat to be roughly five million), the Islamization of some metropolitan areas is the most visible sign of a rampant multiculturalism. But it is hardly the only sign. In France, as in all European countries, Islamization is bound up with a more general phenomenon, the Americanization of society.

In the medium term multiculturalism will have the consequence, as in the United States, of eroding the protections of the welfare state by replacing national solidarity with sectarian loyalties—and this mainly to the advantage of a dominant class that for decades has been looking to disencumber itself of a redistributive system it considers to be unreasonably generous. The effects of this transfer of allegiance have already begun to make themselves felt on working-class perceptions of the proper role of the state, as one recent poll indicates. Whereas a majority feels that "in order to have social justice, it is necessary to take from the rich and give to the poor," 60 percent of manual workers (who are themselves well acquainted with the hardships of unemployment) feel that "the unemployed could find work if they really wanted to."[41] Still more surprisingly, 71 percent of workers and 73 percent of low-wage employees think that "society is going too far in the direction of public assistance." The apparent paradox is explained by the unspoken belief that public assistance primarily benefits immigrants—hence the willingness of the traditional working class to place limits on solidarity. Although its members continue to support a redistributive system in principle, they are now prey to the resentments that a globalized and multicultural society cannot help but arouse among the native poor. In the same 2016 poll, 62 percent of employees and 55 percent of workers agreed that "in order to stimulate growth, it is necessary to keep the role of the state in the French economy to a minimum and to give business as much freedom as possible"—higher percentages than in the case of executives.

As a result of globalization, then, the worst off are led to express inegalitarian free-market sentiments while at the same time remaining committed to the ideal of equality and redistribution. If there is any hope that priority will continue to be attached to preserving the welfare state and defending the principle of secularism in the future, it will be necessary to take a hard and honest look at what it means to be an American society with a republican past.

3

The Management of Public Opinion

How could the egalitarian republican model have given way so quickly to an inegalitarian American model? Why did a society in which the position of the winners from globalization is reinforced every day at the expense of the losers not witness the collapse of its political system? The smooth transition from one regime to another, which has occurred not only in France but in all developed countries, would have been impossible were it not for a concerted attempt by the powers that be to manage public opinion.

This campaign was intended to do two things: first, to maintain the myth of a majority middle class in order to obscure the emergence of an enlarged and economically vulnerable working class; second, to shape perceptions of the areas lying outside the major urban centers in such a way that the lives of the working class in peripheral France will be invisible to everyone else. In order to protect the imaginary land presided over by the French elite, where people of modest means do not exist, alternative perceptions—above all ones that expose the reality of class conflict—have to be refuted at once and, if need be, dismissed as a kind of fascist propaganda. The rhetoric of openness, to others and to the world, constitutes a first line of defense.

Everywhere in the Western world, working-class dissatisfaction with the consequences of globalization is treated as evidence of racism. But racism is not really the issue. In the United States, for example, if Wall Street[1] and Silicon Valley[2] opposed the candidacy of Donald Trump in the 2016 presidential election, it was not because they were offended by his nativist prejudices, any more than they were by his ridiculous coiffure; what they objected to was his willingness to challenge the orthodoxy of free trade (particularly the treaties with Mexico and China) and to call for curbs on immigration.

The Blurring of Class Differences

In the authorized version of contemporary social reality, the middle class survives intact. Almost two decades after sociologists had showed that it was imploding,[3] the expulsion from its ranks of a majority of the people who once composed it is virtually complete.[4] Hopes of upward social mobility have been all but dashed for a whole segment of society. The sociologist Régis Bigot reckons that, in the 1960s, it took about a dozen years on average for members of the middle class to attain the same standard of living as the affluent.[5] Today it takes thirty-five years, and then only if all goes well and no unfortunate incident interferes with the course of a professional career. An entire working life may not be long enough to see one's living conditions improve; indeed, if things do not go well, they may actually deteriorate. The prospect of being forced to climb down the social ladder is now a constant preoccupation for most newcomers to the labor force: although children of the working class remain the least likely to be promoted to higher positions, "downward [career] trajectories are also common for children from the middle class."[6] Because social advancement is blocked by the widening gap between education levels and the qualifications required for better-paying jobs, only inheritors and the children of business executives and senior members of the liberal professions can expect to come out ahead. The question arises, then, if the majority middle class bequeathed by the three decades of rapid economic growth following the Second World War, a socially and politically integrated class whose children were assured of upward social mobility, if this class has disappeared, why does it still live on in official rhetoric and academic analysis?

The determination to keep a defunct socioeconomic category alive at all costs conceals a fundamental political calculation. Widespread belief in the myth of a middle class that still includes two out of three French, as it did during the *Trente Glorieuses*,[7] makes it possible to maintain the illusion that economic and social policies benefit a majority of the population. By implication, then, the working class no longer exists, or else, at most, it is an insignificant minority. The media's habit of referring to the impoverished and violence-prone banlieues as the only "working-class neighborhoods" in the country bolsters this perception, with the happy result that the present "crisis" can be confined to the suburbs of the major cities.

Today the feeling of belonging to the middle class is no longer associated with an aspiration to upward mobility or a certain standard of living but with a desire to set oneself apart from another France— the France of the banlieues. On the one hand, there is a large, predominantly urban middle class; on the other, a small, suburban working class mostly made up of immigrants.[8] This way of looking at the situation allows the socioeconomic question to be reduced to an ethnocultural divergence: on the one side, an integrated white middle class; on the other, a disgruntled working class composed of ethnic minorities. This in turn makes it possible to sustain the fantasy of a majority middle class while ensuring the continuing invisibility of the losers from globalization.

Globalization's winners, though jointly they form a class of power and privilege, can therefore conveniently be lumped together with everyone else. Everyone who matters is in the middle class now: executives and other high earners, skilled workers, salaried personnel, retirees in general, whether well-off or poor.[9] As a psychological matter, this sleight of hand can be performed all the more effortlessly because the poorer elements of society—industrial workers, low-level employees, small farmers, agricultural workers—disappeared from the radar screens of the media and the political class long ago. With the advent of an invisible upper class and an invisible working class, the blurring of class distinctions is complete.

Substituting the agreeable notion of cultural difference for the harsh reality of class conflict has enabled the upper classes to strengthen their hold over the public imagination by adopting a benevolent attitude toward immigration that certifies their moral superiority without threatening their own interests. In the meantime a historic shift has taken place, not only in France but in all the developed countries. A majority of wage earners have fallen out of the middle class. No one but they seem to have noticed.

The official perception of a society divided between the rich (1 percent of the total population), a minority of poor people,[10] and a majority middle class usefully distracts attention from the reality that its foundations are crumbling. Look at median income, social mobility, and residential patterns, however, and it becomes plain that inequalities between manual workers, low-wage employees, and agricultural laborers, young and old alike, and their more prosperous fellow citizens have continued to grow.

Attacking the rich and railing against the concentration of capital in a few hands permits the better off, in spite of their stated belief that French society has no choice but to adapt to demands of the new global economy, to reaffirm their membership in the middle class. Courageously, they denounce the fact that 1 percent of the world's population owns 50 percent of its wealth and that the financial and property holdings of the richest 1 percent will soon exceed those of the remaining 99 percent.[11] Who would say they are wrong to do so?

However objectionable gross disparities in the distribution of wealth and property may be, in France or anywhere else, it is nonetheless wholly illegitimate to use this state of affairs to pretend that class relations no longer exist. The hyperaccumulation of capital does not imply that the richest 1 percent are the only ones to profit from globalization. The system also depends, as I say, on ongoing support from the handsomely remunerated business executives and senior members of the liberal professions who make up much of the rest of the upper half.

Very often the critique of global capitalism is nothing more than a pose that enables the new bourgeoisie to hide the violence of class conflict. François Hollande was not really the enemy of finance, as we know now, any more than the Socialist Party itself was. In December 2016, for example, a bill that would have made corporate tax liability more open to public inspection and debate in France was rejected (with the government's blessing) by a majority of parliamentary deputies, Socialists included. Apparently radical protests against "the rich," against "capital," against "finance" are part of the innately dishonest culture of the new bourgeoisie, allowing it to claim a monopoly on legitimate dissent. Contrary to what the philosopher Raymond Aron imagined,[12] Marxism is no longer really the opium of the intellectuals and still less that of the upper classes. The Marxism-lite that is fashionable among the well-to-do today denies the very existence of class conflict; in this little charade, bravely speaking out against the system is in fact an integral element of the system itself.

In the same way that the new bourgeoisie extolls the virtues of the open society while segregating itself socially, in the same way that it urges everyone to get along while erecting invisible barriers that the wrong sort of people cannot cross, so too it fulminates against capitalism while endorsing economic and social reforms aimed at strengthening it. This is a win-win strategy: it permits globalization's winners to lay claim to disproportionate shares of wealth and property while at the same time presenting themselves not only as rebels but actually as members of an exploited class. Not the least of the advantages of the picture of a France neatly divided into three parts—the rich above, immigrants below, and a vast middle class in between—is that it does away with most of the working class. It hides the fact that since the beginning of the present century the upper classes have been gaining income while manual and nonmanual workers have been losing it. Since 2012, moreover, income disparities have gotten worse, something not seen since the 1930s.[13]

The anti-rich stance of the new bourgeoisie has done nothing to improve the lot of globalization's losers. This comes as no surprise to the invisible poor in France, who remain unconvinced of upper-class sincerity, to say the least. It is not by chance that political organizations proclaiming their determination to change the system, not only the Socialist Party but also smaller parties on the extreme left, attract few listeners among the working class; their main audience is drawn from the upper classes of the large global cities.

In one sense, of course, there is nothing odd about members of the new bourgeoisie finding fault with the rich. After all, they do actually know them. They are integrated with the rich in the same globalized society, and their paths often cross in the major cities. Furthermore, they are rivals, at least potentially. The top earners who preside over the country's economic and cultural life are overshadowed only by a far smaller ruling class that holds real financial power. For the working poor, by contrast, this world of wealth and influence is not merely remote; it is scarcely more than an abstract concept. Unlike the higher social orders, they never come into contact with the rich in their daily lives. What is more—and this is what sets them apart from the higher orders—the "ordinary decent people" that Orwell spoke for do not aspire to social and cultural domination; they want only a decent life.[14] Although they have no personal experience of financial security, much less control, they are acutely aware of the existence of a closed society, an exclusive world whose members work diligently to advance their own interests (not least, the interest that outsiders remain outsiders) and go on, as they have done for decades, promoting the myth of an open, inclusive society.

The capitalist system holds together because it places a substantial corporate and professional class in a position to benefit from the effects of globalization and metropolization. No matter how bitterly the members of this new bourgeoisie of the center left and center right may complain, they nonetheless support and carry out economic and social policies that ultimately are decided by the very wealthy 1 percent and the banks under their control. The system is all the more durable as it has been able up until now to disarm and assimilate its chief critics.

The entire political class, irrespective of party, is emphatically opposed to the ongoing financialization of the economy. Denouncing banks and the tax havens whose advantages they exploit on behalf of their wealthiest clients is a familiar ritual by this point. Just as Hollywood, a creature of multinational corporations, finances films that excoriate the predatory behavior of Wall Street, so too the press, owned by large media companies for the most part, decries corporate control as a threat to editorial independence. The Panama Papers,[15] hailed as a landmark in the growing resistance to an oppressive global order, were financed (directly or indirectly) by US organizations and aided by US newspapers in which powerful conglomerates hold a controlling share.[16] The worldwide publicity generated by the affair was meant to create the impression of a general willingness on the part of the fourth estate to speak truth to power. It may be doubted, however, that Delaware's status as America's premier tax haven is in any way threatened. Today's media circus should remind us that criticism of the financial system is as old as capitalism itself. The original Panama scandal, which brought to light corruption among French journalists and politicians, dates from 1892. Charles Ponzi's famous pyramid scheme, which inspired Bernard Madoff in the 1990s, was devised in 1920. All of this was memorably described forty years ago by the historian Fernand Braudel, who distinguished between a market economy (in which the competitive mechanisms of supply and demand exert a stabilizing influence) and finance (a disruptive force insofar as its reach escapes the control of national jurisdictions).[17] The upper classes today have still less to fear than before, since metropolization and the offshoring of domestic production have given birth to a system in which the interests of the least well-off are no longer represented. In this regard it is worth noting, however, that if the Panama Papers made little or no impression on international markets, the reassertion of popular sovereignty in Great Britain in June 2016 sent tremors through the European ruling class.

In the meantime, social cleavages between the rich and the poor in France (whose number has increased by eight hundred thousand since 2008), and more generally between upper and lower income groups, have continued to widen. In mid-2008, 3 million people were registered as unemployed in France. By the beginning of 2015, the number had risen to 5.3 million, an increase of 70 percent; and of this number, executives accounted only for 8 percent, as against some 70 percent made up by workers and low-wage employees. Far from what the myth of an integrated and majority middle class would lead one to expect, inequalities between a prospering higher France and a struggling lower France have grown larger, not smaller. The confusion created by the catch-all term "middle class," which conflates upper and lower classes, is still more visible when one considers actual living standards. In 2011, only 20 percent of households enjoyed a standard of living higher than €2,177 per month for a single person, €4,280 for a couple with no children, and €5,567 for a couple with two children; for the working class, the figures were €1,183, €2,251, and €3,122, respectively.[18]

These figures make it clear that a substantial part of the population of the major cities belongs not to the middle class but to the upper class. By denouncing the rich and promoting the false idea that the poor live exclusively in the "working-class neighborhoods" of the banlieues, the new bourgeoisie is able to blur the perception of social reality by claiming to be part of the middle class. It is a sort of magic trick: by imagining a society with the richest at the top and the poorest at the bottom, and the upper class smuggled into a notionally predominant class between the two, a majority of the working-class population has been made to vanish. The advantage of this is that it now becomes possible to market metropolization as a regime that benefits the greatest number. The truth of the matter is very different. Under cover of utilitarian rationality, metropolization imposes an inegalitarian model—the preferred model of international finance. The map of the major cities is a map of the world as seen by the largest corporations, not as it is seen by small and medium-sized firms, much less by the working class.

The crudely simplistic view of metropolization as a generally positive social phenomenon fits beautifully with the picture of a comprehensive middle class. Adopted by the whole of the media and most of the academic world, it is a picture of the best of all possible worlds, a world in which a majority of the population is employed by a global economy whose blessings are evenly distributed throughout the country. This view has been reinforced by another gross oversimplification. In 2016, INSEE—France's national statistics bureau—introduced a program for reorganizing local and regional administration that pleased the two major parties of the center left and center right. France is now officially partitioned into fourteen metropolises and thirteen megaregions. It is important to emphasize that territorial reform was never the object of any real debate. For decades both the left and the right had accepted the idea that the country's future should depend on the dynamism of those areas that were best adapted to a global economy. This in turn meant accepting that the time of peripheral France was past.

Peripheral France Does Not Exist

Managing social perceptions, in its territorial aspect, is subordinate to the larger purpose of legitimizing the economic and social policies of the dominant classes by making the working classes effectively invisible. The preponderance of the major cities in the approved way of thinking makes it all the easier to enforce a metropolitan conception of French demography: on the one hand, the rich and their upper-class allies (the latter now cleverly disguised as part of the middle class); on the other, the immigrant working class of the banlieues. Exit the members of the working class who do not live in the largest urban areas.

Any attempt to describe a peripheral France—the forgotten land of small and medium-sized cities and rural areas, home to most of the working class—inevitably brings globalization's losers back into view.

Contrary to the orthodox view, peripheral France does in fact exist; indeed, it is even peopled by "inhabitants,"[19] who form a majority of the nation's population and whose unnoticed presence in all parts of the country conceals the outlines of a new electoral map that threatens to overturn the existing political order. This is the nightmare of the dominant classes. Peripheral France is no less a product of globalization than peripheral America, peripheral England, peripheral Sweden, and peripheral Holland, all very real places where the result of several decades of adaptation to an inegalitarian economic regime has been aggravated suffering and distress. It therefore must be made to disappear from public consciousness.

Act I: The Delegitimization of Working-Class Grievances

The dominant classes consider the working class to be located in the banlieues (more precisely, the so-called sensitive urban zones), where the population is made up by and large of poor immigrants, and in what are called working-class neighborhoods. By reducing the working class to a collection of minority groups it becomes possible, first, to convert a social category into an ethnocultural one, and then to blur both the class relation between upper- and lower-income brackets and the economic disparity between people who live in the largest cities and people who do not.

INSEE, which divides the country into urban and rural areas, provides a useful method for comparing population densities and residential patterns, but it gives only a partial view of working-class society. The urban environment of small and medium-sized cities has almost nothing in common with that of the great metropolitan areas. A Parisian bobo and a worker in Dunkirk, though they both live in cities, plainly lead very different lives. By contrast, a worker in

Dunkirk and someone living in rural Normandy, for example, feel the effects of globalization in much the same way, experience the same kinds of anxiety and insecurity. Rural workers share with the inhabitants of minor urban centers an economic and social reality that is masked by INSEE's categories.

The restrictive definition of rural France is evidently a political ruse. It marginalizes areas that in reality are far larger than INSEE assumes by suggesting that members of the working class who do not live in cities (read: the largest cities) are an elderly and vanishing minority. The simmering discontent of rural France has never really been taken seriously. And yet, as a recent government report acknowledges, "places where it takes more than twenty minutes to reach local health-care facilities are all in rural areas, and problems of accessibility are likely to become more serious in the next ten years because of the aging of the population."[20]

Unlike INSEE's way of dividing up the country, the concept of a peripheral France encompasses very different areas whose common characteristic is that they are more or less distant from the most dynamic centers of job creation, the main metropolitan areas. It has the advantage of unifying categories that until now have been opposed to one another: industrial workers, low-wage employees in both the public and private sectors, small farmers, agricultural workers—all these people, young and old alike, are of one mind about the negative effects of globalization. The idea of a peripheral France, mostly working class, that accounts for roughly 60 percent of the nation's population is disconcerting precisely because it contradicts the dominant conception. As we have seen, its definition is perfectly straightforward, however often it may be mischaracterized, willfully or otherwise.

The first error of interpretation confuses peripheral France with the nation's urban peripheries,[21] which is to say a marginal territory comprising only 20 percent of the population, much of it the home-owning lower-middle class. These two Frances are not at all the same. Conflating them makes it possible to treat the people who live in peripheral France as belonging to the "middle class." The geographer Laurent Chalard demonstrated long ago, however, that the urban perimeter is by no means homogeneous: in addition to the communities of a "chosen" rim voluntarily inhabited by the upper classes (the prosperous suburbs in the department of Yvelines, west of Paris, are a classic example), there is also an "enforced" rim in which persons of modest means are concentrated for want of any better alternative (the poor suburbs in the department of Seine-et-Marne, east of Paris, for instance).[22] This confusion is all the more absurd as the population of the urban perimeter is not overrepresented in peripheral France: like the nation's overall population, 40 percent live in the largest metropolitan areas and 60 percent in peripheral France.

The effect of making the working class of peripheral France coincide with the residents of the urban perimeter is to delegitimize protest from below. Workers, employees, small farmers, agricultural laborers—all the losers from globalization are conveniently relocated in the home-owning lower-middle class. The social question disappears, allowing opponents of the dominant economic and social model to be described as members of the lower-middle class. In this form of political/psychological warfare, it is essential that people living in the countryside be kept in their place, which is to say the lands occupied by a minority that grows ever older and less significant. INSEE reckons the rural population to be a more or less small proportion of the total, between 5 and 20 percent. The working poor who live outside the major cities are therefore considered to constitute a structural minority.

Elected officials in rural districts, on both the left and the right, trapped by a statistical prejudice that minimizes and stigmatizes their constituents, have a very hard time making the rest of the country understand that they are not only the defenders of the "Gallic village" and its way of life; they are also the natural representatives of a working class that is much larger than is commonly supposed and the advocates of a kind of economic development that is complementary to that of the major cities. Counting the residents of the small and medium-sized cities, these officials speak for a majority of the working-class population. The challenge they face—finding a way to combat a concerted attempt to associate these areas in the public mind with a closed France (and, by contrast, the major cities with an open France) and so to legitimize metropolization by delegitimizing working-class grievances—should not be underestimated. And yet a rising wave of social and cultural protest in recent years has had some effect: rural society is no longer completely hidden from view, forcing government officials at least to recognize the existence of a peripheral France—a small but nonetheless telling victory, even if it has not yet had any major political consequence.

The great majority of local elected officials (from mayors to departmental deputies in the National Assembly) are competent and well aware of the difficulties confronting them, but they are often without power in their own party. As representatives of the areas that are most deeply affected by globalization, they remain subject to the will of party higher-ups who oblige them to support economic policies and territorial reforms that worsen the situation of their constituents. Notwithstanding that they have been elected to defend the interests of places where the middle class is being hollowed out, they are instructed to parrot a party line based on the idea of an integrated and majority middle class. The elected officials of peripheral France now have their backs to the wall: if they do not wish to surrender to the National Front, they have no choice but to rise up against the party leadership. Are they prepared to go that far? What price would they have to pay in the event their revolt is unsuccessful?

Act II: The Instrumentalization of Poverty

The concept of a peripheral France reflects an economic and social reality that is obvious to a majority of the French people: the everyday experience of the small and medium-sized cities and rural areas where they live and work, if they are not unemployed. In order to discredit the idea of a struggling and increasingly impoverished working class, the champions of the existing system instrumentalize the question of poverty.

The figures in INSEE's annual surveys unambiguously establish that a majority of the "working class" and the "poor" live in peripheral France. Obviously this does not mean that there are not members of the working class or poor people in the major metropolitan areas; it means that they constitute a minority in these places. There is nothing surprising about this: gentrification in the largest cities has excluded the poor and people of modest means for decades. Only a fraction of these categories—the immigrant working class—still lives there, mainly in public housing projects or in substandard private housing. This statistical reality is nonetheless not immune to shameless manipulation.

It will be recalled that members of economically and socially disadvantaged populations do not necessarily qualify as poor, though in some cases the two categories may overlap; in any event, the ordinary worker is not poor by definition. INSEE's analysis, by contrast, is concerned solely with people whose income falls below a certain officially designated threshold, which is to say a fraction of the working class, whose geographical distribution is not the same as that of the working class taken as a whole. INSEE's principle of selection lays exclusive emphasis on those areas in which poverty is most heavily concentrated, the urban cores of metropolitan areas (most of which are located, by the way, in peripheral France). The official analysis has nothing to say about a much larger population, all those people who live slightly above the poverty line but who are at risk of rapidly slipping into poverty at any moment.

The confusion is compounded by a highly elastic criterion for ranking metropolitan areas by size. According to INSEE's definition, a city may be identified as a large metropolitan area (consisting of an urban core and its suburbs) if it supports at least ten thousand jobs.[23] This remarkably low threshold implies that a majority of the small and medium-sized cities of peripheral France qualify as large metropolitan areas. INSEE's typology is useful for comparing population densities on a national scale. The problem is that it standardizes urban experience: the urban core, banlieues, and other parts of the suburban periphery are thus considered to be identical, no matter where they are located in France. This method presents a particular difficulty in relation to the urban cores of metropolitan areas, whose demographic character greatly varies both within and across regions.

To group Paris together with a city such as Saint-Quentin, north of the capital in Picardy, makes no sense. Paris, or at least the city proper, accounts for less than 20 percent of the population of its metropolitan area (2.2 million of 12 million inhabitants, in 2010); whereas Saint-Quentin makes up very nearly half of the population of its metropolitan area (53,000 of 111,000 inhabitants).[24] On a national scale, INSEE's methodology leads to the uninformative, if not actually ridiculous, conclusion that there are 241 large metropolitan areas in France, which jointly account for 83 percent of the total population! This amounts to putting the very largest metropolitan areas (Paris,

Lyon, Marseille, Bordeaux, Lille, and so on) on the same level with much smaller cities like Châteaudun, Guingamp, Tergnier, and so on. It should be noted that these small cities, and the poor who live there, are part of peripheral France, even if INSEE considers them to be urban centers.

The concept of a metropolitan area gets misused in another way as well. In asserting that the rate of poverty in a metropolitan area is typically higher in the urban core (16 percent on average) than in its outlying districts (roughly 10 percent), a crucial distinction between "urban" and "suburban" is elided. The fact of the matter is that a substantial part of peripheral France is urban and that a substantial part of the nation's urban peripheries (the wealthy suburbs) comes within the orbit of the largest cities. Claims that the rate of poverty is almost always higher in the urban core therefore dishonestly reaffirm the dominant perception, namely, that French society is divided between the disadvantaged populations of the banlieues of major cities and the integrated middle class that inhabits all other areas, suburban and rural alike.

Troubled metropolitan communities and neighborhoods do, of course, contain a large number of poor households, but this in no way disposes of the fact that a majority of working-class and poor households reside in peripheral France. It is an inconvenient fact because it poses an insurmountable obstacle to the ideological campaign being conducted on the basis of an incomplete and oversimplified picture of the nation's socioeconomic geography to divert attention from the increasingly bleak outlook for the working class.

Once the crude division of the country into cities and countryside is accepted, it becomes a simple matter to place an overriding emphasis on urban poverty while minimizing the severity and extent of rural poverty. When the demonstrable existence of rural poverty is in fact acknowledged, it is falsely claimed to affect only retired persons and the elderly, as opposed to the impoverished young people of the "neighborhoods." No one disputes that the immigrant residents of the public housing projects in such neighborhoods are poor. Why should it be impossible to recognize the reality of widespread poverty and economic insecurity in peripheral France?

The gross oversimplification of the phenomenon of poverty, and the disingenuous stereotyping that accompanies it, do not suggest any particularly benevolent intent on the part of the dominant classes. To the contrary, their aim is to restrict the social question to the banlieues. By implanting in the public mind a reductive and exclusionary perception of poverty, it becomes possible to redirect the focus of public policy to a limited set of urban areas and target populations, this as a prelude to the gradual dismantling of the welfare state. A class strategy of this sort is bound to stir up resentment among people who no longer figure in the calculations of policy makers, people who feel that they have been shunted aside now that official concern for the plight of the banlieues (read: "immigrants") has exhausted the government's capacity for self-interested displays of compassion. This in turn allows opinion leaders to encourage the related perception of peripheral France, and particularly of its rural inhabitants, as "closed-minded," "embittered," and "racist."

A way out from this pointless exercise in competitive victimization could easily be found if the authorities were to accept one simple fact, that today the working class as a whole is adversely affected by globalization. Looking at a measure of the population in terms of economic instability such as the one sketched in the appendix—a fragility index I developed in collaboration with the geographer Christophe Noyè in constructing the concept of peripheral France—it becomes clear that the disadvantaged live not only in the major cities but also in a great many places outside them. The poor are both urban and rural; they live in cities, big and small, as well as in the country-side; they are old, middle-aged, and young. What they have in com-mon is that they overwhelmingly belong to the working class. Breaking free from the caricatural conception of poverty that forms the basis of current policy will be possible only if we put the social question back at the center of debate.

The Ideology of the Superstore

Metropolization, as the geographer Gérard-François Dumont has pointed out, is above all an ideology. Like every ideology, it is the product of concerted effort: a great part of the academic world, the media, and the political class purvey the same conception of society, the same view of local and regional organization, the same globalized economic model. Like every ideology, it rests on a system of fixed ideas that depends in turn on the unexamined assumption that France is largely "urban." Dumont argued that this notion is deliberately in-tended to marginalize the rest of the country, "rural" France, whose inhabitants have been reduced in INSEE's calculation to 15–20 per-cent of the total population.[25] Eurostat, the agency responsible for publishing the official statistics of the European Union, implicitly concurs with Dumont, putting the actual rate of urbanization in France at 41.7 percent[26]—scarcely half the figure of 80 percent arrived at by INSEE. But reality counts for little in the face of ideology.

Metropolization can therefore be described as a progressive and positive process. The negative effects are passed over in silence, not least the fact that the major cities are expensive. In Dumont's account-ing, "Higher per capita allocation of state funds, a clearly stronger re-lationship between the number of local civil servants and the number

of inhabitants, considerable expenditures on urban renewal, pollu-
tion, traffic congestion, safety problems, overcrowded public spaces,
deterioration of public services, erosion of the common interest."[27]
Add to this the fact that, in the global metropolises, social cleavages
conceal potentially uncontrollable ethnic and cultural pressures: in
France, as in all developed countries, tensions in the major cities lead
at regular intervals to acts of violence and more or less serious public
disturbances.

It is of little importance that the rate of voting participation is
lowest in the largest metropolitan areas. Big, the dominant classes
have decided, is beautiful.[28] But just as the concentration of retail activity in large chain stores that are typically located outside downtown
business districts has brought about the disappearance of small shop
owners, the globalized metropolitan economic model has led to a loss
of jobs and reduced commerce in the smaller cities. Territorial reform,
and with it the downgrading of the last visible administrative unit of
peripheral France, the department, testify to the shutting down of
democratic debate. Opposing voices are silenced. Yesterday the defenders of small business were accused of fascism; today the defenders
of small towns and cities, and more generally of the French countryside, are accused of Pétainism.[29]

Merely mentioning "peripheral France" is now treated as a repre-
hensible attempt to set poor whites against the immigrants of the
banlieues; taking notice of the problems that rural communities face
is treated as evidence of a desire to rehabilitate France's disgraceful
fascist and anti-Dreyfusard past, to remind the French that "the land
does not lie."[30] The invocation of a perfectly meaningless Vichyist
catchphrase (the land does not lie any more than it tells the truth)
makes it possible to immediately discredit any argument that takes
into account the actual social and cultural experience of a class that

nonetheless constitutes a majority of the French people. In much the same way, it is suggested that calling attention to the cleavage between peripheral France and metropolitan France is somehow synonymous with espousing isolationism.

We have come full circle: to talk about peripheral France and/or the rural working class today is tantamount to longing for a return to the dark days of Vichy. It does not matter that peripheral France in no way corresponds to the rural France of the early 1940s; that the economic sociology of peripheral France in no way coincides with the economic sociology of rural France in the early 1940s; that, to the contrary, peripheral France is where manual workers and low-wage employees in the service sector live; that it is as much urban as it is rural; that, far from being the victim of a rural exodus, it is the beneficiary of an urban exodus—the essential thing is to stigmatize unwelcome opinions and shut down free debate. Confronted with criticism rooted in facts rather than ideology, and lacking any coherent plan to improve the lives of the inhabitants of peripheral France, sacrificed on the altar of metropolization, the dominant classes have now taken to vilifying their critics as fascists.

Antifascism as a Class Weapon

The social and cultural relegation of the French working class portends a major political crisis. Growing anger at official neglect of peripheral France and the new spirit of radicalism it has generated represent a formidable challenge to the present socioeconomic system. The dominant classes evidently believe that the threat to their authority is so great that they have no choice but to deploy their ultimate weapon: antifascism. Unlike the antifascism of the last century, it is not concerned with combating an authoritarian regime or a single-party state. As the Italian filmmaker Pier Paolo Pasolini rightly suspected more than forty years ago, analyzing the new strategy adopted by the left with the abandonment of its historical commitment to the working class and the cause of social struggle, "a facile antifascism" would soon be "aimed at an archaic fascism that no longer exists and that will never exist [again]."[31] And so it came to pass. The French left's great campaign of resistance against the looming menace was launched a decade later, with its turn to the right under Mitterrand in 1983.

Lionel Jospin, Socialist prime minister from 1997 to 2002, later acknowledged not only that the campaign was "just a put-on" but that "the National Front has never been a fascist party."[32] It is not by chance that the instigators and financiers of antiracism and antifascism are also among the most enthusiastic promoters of the global economic system. From the philosopher and media celebrity Bernard-Henri Lévy to the late fashion magnate Pierre Bergé, from the corporate media to the companies of the CAC 40, from Hollywood to Canal Plus, the upper classes rushed to embrace the cause of resistance. "¡No pasarán!"[33] suddenly became the rallying cry of the prevailing economic interests and the public intellectuals who speak for them, on both the left and the right. It is interesting to note, by the way, as the independent researcher Jacques Leclerq has done,[34] that antifascist groups (whose violent attacks on the police during the demonstrations against the proposed labor-reform law in 2016 attracted particular attention) recruit mainly from among young bourgeois university graduates.[35]

One aspect of antifascism's usefulness as a class weapon is of special interest. It allows distrusted elites to reclaim the moral high ground by treating all criticism of the effects of globalization as proof of hateful motives. In order to be a lastingly effective strategy, however, the fascist enemy has to be made into a permanent obsession—hence the saturation coverage of the National Front in the media. The struggle against fascism is therefore waged today by promoting fascism, by building it up—a perversely protracted fight to the death whose purpose is not to destroy the enemy, but to ensure its indefinite survival. It is not the National Front, a party of small and medium-sized businesses, that influences the working class; it is the other way around. The National Front is merely a symptom of the working class's unequivocal rejection of the global system. The target of today's fashionable antifascism is not the National Front; it is the working class, which must be tarred with fascism in order to discredit the complaints of a lower France infected by the disease of "populism." Implicit in this term is the suggestion that poor people are not intelligent enough to understand how globalization enriches their daily lives, and that for this very reason they are easily manipulated.

Bernard-Henri Lévy is supposed to have demolished the sovereignist argument by exposing its roots in nationalist (read: fascist) fanaticism. Dissent from globalization, direct or indirect, whether it takes the form of Euroskepticism or a repudiation of free-market dogma or push-back against the effects of deregulation, is inadmissible. Sovereignism, Lévy tells us, is pure foolishness, idiocy—in a word, crap.

Merely to describe the social and cultural insecurity experienced by the working class is to "play into the hands" of the fascists. The need for self-censorship is regularly insisted on: one should not say certain things, even though they are true, because to do so would serve only to assist and abet the forces of evil—a perfect illustration of what Pasolini called the "fascism of antifascism."[36] From the point of view of the dominant classes, the stakes could not be greater. If they lose the war of perceptions, they will be forced finally to confront the social question and to assume responsibility for economic and social policies that have taken a terrible toll on the working class. It is in this light that the new McCarthyism practiced by "free-market Godwinians" is to be understood.[37]

For the dominant classes, even the defense of the traditional values of mutual aid and solidarity is suspect. The philosopher Jean-Claude Michéa, for having done nothing more than echo Orwell in speaking of the "common decency of ordinary people," found his name added to the list of dangerous "reactionaries" (another synonym for "fascist")—the list, in other words, of those who play into the hands of evildoers.[38] The same treatment is reserved for scholars and researchers who dare to propose another way of looking at the predicament of ordinary people. From the demographer Michèle Tribalat to the philosopher Michel Onfray, the catalogue of those who have been traduced as propagandists for the extreme right grows ever longer as the legitimacy of the dominant classes continues to be eroded. One could easily multiply examples, but the method is always the same: anyone who tries to give a true picture of working-class life is smeared as an enemy of civilized society.

The dominant classes are aware that they are losing the war of perceptions. Panic has begun to set in. Whole territories are now reviled as bastions of fascism. Peripheral France itself is maligned as the product of a xenophobic white imagination filled with hatred for the ethnic neighborhoods of the banlieues. It makes no difference that the distinction between rural areas and small and medium-sized cities, on the one hand, and the large metropolitan areas, on the other, has never rested on an ethnic cleavage; that peripheral France, which includes the nation's overseas administrative departments and territories, is not ethnically and culturally homogeneous. The primary aim is to demean and censure the grim places where the working class hides out from the world, by invidious contrast with the welcoming and open-minded atmosphere of the major cities. As against isolationist

France, the bleak garrison of ignorant provincials and bigoted rustics, there is cosmopolitan France, the blessed land of enlightenment, prosperity, and cultural tolerance. But make no mistake, the new bourgeoisie that peddles this line has no interest whatsoever in protecting "immigrants," "Muslims," or "minorities" from the imminent threat of fascism. Its chief objective is to defend its own class interests.

Using antifascism as a weapon makes it possible in the medium term to discredit alternative economic policies while containing working-class protest. At the same time, however, it reveals the growing isolation of the dominant classes. The days when a strategy of fear of this sort could be counted on to keep the plebs in line, whether in peripheral France or in the banlieues, are over. The working class no longer speaks the language of the intelligentsia. The "theater of the antifascist struggle" is now acted out in empty houses throughout the country.[39]

Not only is creating a climate of fear no longer effective as a strategy of class defense, it is now beginning to be turned against the very people who for so long have used it to their own advantage. The determination of the dominant classes to polarize public debate still further, setting "racists" against "antiracists" and "fascists" against "antifascists," signals a cowardly retreat in the face of gathering resistance to a model they are unwilling or unable to defend. On both the left and the right, the bourgeoisie finds itself tempted by the prospect of a one-party state. Whether or not intellectuals are much more inclined to totalitarianism than ordinary people are, as Simon Leys suggested thirty years ago,[40] it is all the more appealing to a ruling class that is in grave danger of losing the war of perceptions—and with it the last shreds of their own legitimacy.

When ideological abuse is no longer enough for the higher France to turn election results in its favor, when heaping scorn on the heads of those who are brave enough to demand an end to the status quo is no longer enough to silence them, the willingness of those at the top to bar those at the bottom from exercising their democratic rights can no longer be concealed. The argument used—an argument from class and authority that turns on the level of education among the members of the working class—represents a last desperate attempt to reassert political control. In France, the reaction by politicians and intellectuals to the vote by the British working class in June 2016 to leave Europe revealed not only how deeply distrusted they are by the ordinary people who make up the majority of the nation's population, but also how determined they are to restrict the civil rights of anyone who opposes the system they administer on behalf of the ruling class. The businessman and political adviser Alain Minc declared that Brexit "was the victory of uneducated people over educated people."[41] Bernard-Henri Lévy, for his part, saw it as the "victory of the little over the great, of stupidity over the mind."[42] With words such as these, the totalitarian impulse is exposed for all to see. They are the words of mounting panic and despair. The little people of lower France understand this perfectly well. They are no longer willing to allow the terms of political debate to be dictated to them.

4

The Defection of the Working Class

Having broken their chains—the chains of traditional political attachments—the members of the working class refuse any longer to be enslaved by their old political and cultural masters. This great escape[1] heralds the emergence of a countersociety that in every respect is at odds with the economic and social model of the dominant classes. From the banlieues to the lands of peripheral France, the implications of this shift affect everyone who belongs to the working class, regardless of ethnic background or social status. Manual and nonmanual workers, agricultural laborers, minor civil servants, native-born and immigrant French citizens, Muslim and non-Muslim—they have all fled the plantation, and they will not be coming back.

The rejection of politicians on both the right and the left, the turning away from the labor unions, the mistrust of the media, of pundits, and, more generally, of anyone who talks down to the working class—all these things have reached new heights. And yet this show of defiance has so far not produced the momentous upheaval that some political strategists had predicted. The resounding failure of far-left parties among working-class voters proves that people at the bottom are no longer dupes; they realize that the politics of the past have led to a dead end. A long-drawn-out process of political and cultural disaffiliation has now begun. The prospect of winning freedom at long last has inspired the working poor to abandon their old allegiances. This will happen only gradually, though the pace of events will accelerate as more and more of them fall out of the middle class. They no longer expect to be saved by a leader or a party. Nor do they await any longer the revolution that was supposed to be brought about by an alliance between a progressive lower-middle class and the "people." From the banlieues to peripheral France, the working class as a whole is turning its back on a system of representation controlled by politicians, unions, and the media.

This repudiation is an unforeseen consequence of globalization. Neither politicians nor journalists have yet managed to get their heads around a phenomenon that is independent of both traditional bipartisanism and established ideologies. After several decades of increasing economic and social insecurity, the working class no longer recognizes the legitimacy (much less the moral superiority) of its former governors. The reaction of the dominant classes, caught by surprise, has been to ostracize working-class society ever more completely. But it is too late; their authority has ceased to be admitted. The escape of the working class, a result of the hollowing out of the middle class, signals a historic and irreversible shift, nothing less than a mutiny by the lower France against the higher France. This turn of events is described by the dominant classes, of course, as a "withdrawal," an irrational retreat into ethnic hatreds. The reality is otherwise.

There is nothing surprising, really, about the defection of the working poor. This is what happens when a lower class is no longer willing to respect the social and cultural norms imposed by an upper class. The countersociety that is now emerging is not the residue of an ideology or the result of a scheme concocted by a powerful few. It is the consequence of forcing an entire class of people to bear the costs of a system they did not choose. Contrary to what the dominant classes believe, ideas motivate people much less than do the things that happen to them every day. This is particularly true in the case of the working poor, who have borne the brunt of the economic and cultural transformations of the past several decades. Unemployment, job insecurity, stagnant and/or declining incomes, the weakening of the welfare state—these are the things that unite the working class, not ideology. Similarly, it is the advent of a multicultural society that explains the renewed concern with ethnic identity among the disadvantaged members of society, both in peripheral France and in the banlieues, not support for any white nationalist or Islamist program. The separatist feeling that is increasingly perceptible today springs chiefly from a desire to protect a stock of social and cultural capital that has been put at risk by metropolization. Far from buying into the upper-class fantasy of rich and poor living together as one big happy family, the lower class is now determined to take matters into its own hands and put an end to the anxiety and suffering generated by an unjustly inegalitarian socioeconomic system. The territorial reforms of the past several years, which by ensuring the social and residential immobility of the working class confirm its de facto relegation, have done more to transform the political thinking of underprivileged people than any partisan ideology has.

Ensuring the social and residential immobility of the working classes is not the official policy of either of the governing parties. Nevertheless it deepens the divide between metropolitan France and peripheral France; and by restricting career opportunities, particularly for the young, it contradicts one of the fundamental tenets of a globalized society. The working class has no choice but to adapt to this unacknowledged policy of enforced localism as best it can and to find ways of turning its constraints to its own advantage. Localism, in and of itself, is obviously not incompatible with the ideals of openness to others and to the world; and by acting as a counterbalance to the relentless growth of the largest urban centers, it suggests a response to the present ecological crisis while at the same time helping to strengthen social cohesiveness.

There is no point pretending that a united working class exists today. Solidarity in the customary sense has been largely preempted by the economic and social vulnerabilities that affect all of peripheral France. But this has not prevented the first stirrings of a countersociety from making themselves felt; and as the challenge to the global model becomes more organized, a consciousness of class unity will gradually reassert itself. What the dominant classes call the turning inward of the working class is in fact a natural response to a neoliberal society that is inimical to the very notion of solidarity. In seeking to escape a modern form of enslavement that condemns it to social and residential immobility, the working class is not trying to go against the tide of history; it is trying to come to terms with a new economic and territorial regime that threatens its very existence.

The Abandonment of Traditional Attachments

In France's regional elections of 2015, 63 percent of nonmanual workers, 51 percent of manual workers, and 67 percent of the unemployed (most of them belonging to the first two categories) abstained. Of those who did vote, a substantial number cast their ballots for the lists of the National Front: 55 percent of voting manual workers, 37 percent of nonmanual workers, and 33 percent of unemployed. A much smaller number of working-class voters supported the traditional parties: together, the Republicans (and their allies), the Socialist Party (and its allies), the Left Front (FG), and the Greens (EELV) attracted the votes of only 18 percent of the working class.[2]

The parties of the right and the left, which for decades have called on France to fall in step with the forward march of capitalism, are now supported only by the winners from globalization and those who are protected against its harmful consequences. The electorate invariably behaves in the same fashion. The upper classes, from the richest at the very top down to the humblest bobo, massively support one of the two neoliberal parties on the right and the left; those who are able to more or less comfortably weather occasional storms (many of them high-ranking civil servants and their predecessors who have taken retirement) cast their ballots for the same mainstream parties. A majority of the working class, by contrast, from the banlieues to the heartlands of peripheral France, abstain; those who do vote tend to support the party farthest outside the system, the National Front. Only persons above the age of sixty in working-class districts still support the Socialist Party and, to a greater extent, the Republican Party. Contrary to the media cliché that the aging of the French population is an engine of populist protest, it is in fact one of the system's strongest ramparts.[3]

The same pattern of political disaffiliation recurs from one election cycle to the next. Presidential elections are an exception, since working-class turnout for them is higher (usually to the benefit of the National Front); even so, contempt for the political class as a whole is plain. What is more, it is widely shared. Almost three-quarters of the French people today, 72 percent, think that politicians (male and female alike) are "corrupt"; 89 percent believe that they are concerned only with their own personal advantage;[4] 87 percent feel that governments, whether of the left or the right, take no interest in "people like them."[5]

The loss of public trust is not limited to politicians. It includes opinion leaders as a group, above all in the media (only 20 percent of those surveyed believe they tell the truth). Suspicion of journalists is particularly pronounced: more than three-quarters of those surveyed say they do not trust them (only a quarter believe that journalists are "in touch with reality").[6] In a period of mounting economic insecurity, when nearly 55 percent of the population just barely manages to make ends meet every month, polling shows that the French in general, and especially those who make up the lower France, no longer expect anything from the higher France. The great escape is now under way.

The Hollowing Out of the Middle Class

The defection of the working class is not the result, as it is usually said, of unrest or of populism or of a renewed susceptibility to fascist ideology. It is the result of what used to be the bottom layer of the middle class being gradually peeled away and discarded.

Industrial workers, who were the first to feel the effects of globalization and large-scale unemployment, were also the first to enlarge the ranks of both abstentionists and voters for the National Front. From its beginnings as a working-class movement in the 1990s, the National Front has since become the party of all those who have fallen out of the middle class. Little by little, the rest of the low-end categories (other manual workers, office workers and salaried employees of various descriptions, small farmers, agricultural laborers), along with a significant proportion of middle managers, walked away from the major parties, adding further to the number of abstentionists and National Front supporters. Low-wage urban employees were the first to migrate to the National Front, followed by people from the countryside. Like skilled manual workers, these predominantly private-sector members of the labor force, who not so long ago were a part of the traditional middle class, find themselves confronted with job insecurity and a decline (at best, a leveling off) in their standard of living. In the meantime they have been joined by mid- and low-level public servants who see their position threatened by the emergence of a multicultural and increasingly volatile society.

If social and cultural security used to be the cement holding together a now-defunct middle class, social and cultural insecurity is what unites the members of this newly excluded working class, left out from a system of political representation and media publicity that serves the interests of globalization's winners and all those who are shielded from its worst effects. It is this transformation, wrongly seen as a sign of the rightward drift of French society, that explains the flight from the traditional parties on both the left and the right. The underlying dynamic is robust. Barring some presently unforeseeable development, it will only gain momentum as one generation gives way to the next.

Although the aging of the postwar baby-boomer generation continues to work to the advantage of the major parties (particularly on the right, which captures the votes of most working-class retirees),[7] the trend will not last much longer. Older people who remain persuaded of the legitimacy of the existing system and devoted to the ideals of the governing parties will soon be succeeded in retirement by veteran members of the labor force and after that by another generation, still young today, many of them from working-class backgrounds, who are on the front lines of globalization.

With the hollowing out of the middle class, blue-collar workers abandoned the Communist and Socialist left, white-collar workers deserted the governing parties of the center left and right (the "natural" representatives of the middle class), and agricultural workers and others living in rural areas dissociated themselves from the right. The most striking development, however, has certainly been the divorce between the working class and the left. It is an old story by now. Proof that the divorce was final was that it had become necessary to explicitly qualify the term "left" by the phrase "working class" in order to refer to a political orientation dedicated to defending the interests of the least well-off. In the space of a few decades, the old left of the masses had given way to a new bourgeois hashtag left.

The figures are unambiguous, virtually unarguable in fact. In the regional elections of 2015, 45 percent of the working class voted for the National Front, 6 percent for the Left Front, 19 percent for the Socialist Party and its allies, and 16 percent for the Republicans.[8] Among the reasons for working-class disillusionment in the wake of the Socialist Party's swerve to the right in 1983, two stand out: the unintended consequences of "cultural leftism"[9] and the faux critique of free trade. The hypocritical rebellocracy of the educated left, which claims to despise "capital," the "banks," the "market," and the "multinationals" while ceaselessly advocating globalization (so long as it does not harm their own interests), has alienated all but a small fraction of the party's working-class supporters.

The End of Cultural Integration

For a long time, minorities constituted a reliably leftist working-class constituency. That time is over. The inhabitants of the banlieues have now forsworn their traditional political allegiance as well.

For many years the electoral results in the poorest suburbs seemed to suggest that French Muslims were loyal to the parties of the left. This inference was never as well founded as it appeared to be. The reason that leftist municipal governments were typically reelected was that rates of abstention were very high. And when Muslims did turn out in large numbers, as in the presidential elections of 2007 and 2012, it was not because they supported the "values" of the left but because they were determined to prevent a candidate (namely, Sarkozy) whom they considered to be Islamophobic and antiblack from being elevated to the nation's highest office. Muslim voters, representing 5 percent of the total electorate, cast their ballots overwhelmingly (86 percent) for Hollande and thus assured his victory.[10]

All that is ancient history by now. The left's performance in the banlieues in the last municipal, regional, and European elections shows that French Muslims no longer vote for the left in large numbers today, that abstention is the norm, and that, while support for the National Front remains negligible, the center right has nonetheless registered significant gains. In the 2015 regional elections, a majority of Muslim voters stayed away from the polls (nearly 59 percent), ten points higher than the national average.[11] From now on, unless an obviously anti-immigrant or Islamophobic candidate looks to be in a position to win, minorities will no longer reflexively vote for the lists of the left.

The sources of disenchantment among the immigrant working class include the failure of the left's economic policies, secularist social reforms that offend religious sensibilities, and mistrust of a lower-middle class resolved to protect its hard-won gains. Despite certain obvious differences, the motivations of the immigrant working class are at bottom similar to those of low-income whites and other natives of peripheral France. All of them are taking part in the great escape. Young people, in particular, expect something other than the usual rhetoric of compassion and/or victimization. More than anything else, what sets them apart from their parents is a belief in the importance of personal initiative and responsibility. In peripheral France no less than in the banlieues, young people from working-class backgrounds understand that their dreams will not be realized by taking orders from party leaders or political strategists or anyone else who is rolling out the latest model of managed social struggle. No one any longer believes the old revolutionary fantasy of an alliance between the lower-middle class and the working class, least of all in places where the most urgent concern is making ends meet every month. Instead what we are witnessing is the emergence of a generation of young entrepreneurs from immigrant neighborhoods. Neoliberal in outlook, they nonetheless remain attached to traditional values, which inspire them to preserve what they consider to be a precious social and cultural inheritance. They succeed, in other words, in combining Islam and Macron—a far, far cry from outmoded leftist orthodoxy!

On the subject of economic security and immigration control, the left's rhetoric seems almost calculated to unsettle a group of voters who are very concerned about social stability and order. Many of the social reforms sponsored by the left (particularly the legalization of same-sex marriage) have provoked dismay as well. The success of a large-scale campaign urging parents in Muslim neighborhoods to pull their children out of school one day a month, in protest against a government program characterized as an attempt to make gender theory part of the elementary curriculum, shows that the willingness of immigrant families to act on their beliefs can no longer be ignored.[12] This tendency is particularly marked among young and middle-aged people who reject the French secularist ideal of social integration, insisting instead on the right to lay claim to an identity that is bound up with the religion and culture of Islam.

The process of disaffiliation has had the effect of swelling the ranks of the abstentionists in all working-class areas. Rates of abstention among French-born members of the working class, though very high, are nonetheless lower than the average for immigrants. This is no doubt a result of the aggressive promotion of a traditional conception of French identity by the National Front. There is nothing comparable in the banlieues, where the political appeal of an implausible claim to Frenchness remains marginal at best.[13]

The Denial of Democracy

Thanks to a tradition of unkept promises and the permanent alternation of the same two governing parties, the political class has long done its part to degrade and discredit official rhetoric. The 2005 referendum on the European constitutional treaty nonetheless marked a turning point, revealing not only the extent of the cultural divide between politicians and the media, on the one hand, and the members of the working class, on the other, but also the shift toward a truly oligarchical system. Notwithstanding the rejection by the people of the proposed constitution, three years later France ratified a very similar arrangement, the Treaty of Lisbon.

The so-called Polish plumber controversy is a perfect illustration of the chasm that separates a political class enlisted to serve the interests of a global order and the ordinary people who are exposed to its harshest effects. The French working class, already weakened by the new international division of labor, does not wish to see it supplemented by an organized system of social dumping within Europe as a whole. Concerns about "posted workers"—officially defined as employees sent by their employer to provide a particular service in another EU member state on a temporary basis—raised by opponents of the treaty, who feared that such workers would undercut local service providers, were rapidly swept aside on the pretext (for that is evidently what it was) that anyone who opposed the treaty was xenophobic.

The expression "Polish plumber" (a shorthand for all such workers coined by Philippe Val, the former editor in chief of *Charlie*

Hebdo) was first popularized during debate over the treaty by a prominent right-wing politician, Philippe de Villiers, and then taken up by a prominent left-wing politician, Jean-Luc Mélenchon. Supporters of the treaty dismissed the charge of social dumping as a misrepresentation and accused critics of antiforeign prejudice.[14] The fact of the matter, however, is that by permitting workers posted to France to make social security contributions at the prevailing rate in their country of origin, the directive allowed foreign firms to export lower-cost labor, thereby creating a regime of unfair competition that inevitably put French firms at a disadvantage. Not only are the sending employers able to pay these workers the minimum wage, but they have no obligation to offer employee benefits (bonuses, workers' compensation, meal vouchers, and so on). It is therefore very much a matter of legalizing social dumping on a continental scale, and in no way a xenophobic fantasy. The National Commission to Combat Illegal Employment (CNLTI) has recently revealed that the number of posted workers in France increased markedly in the decade after 2005, rising to a level of 286,000 in 2015 (a majority of them Polish, as it happens).[15]

But on this central question, concerning the effects of the international division of labor on the living conditions of the European working class, there has been no debate. Within Europe during this period, income and wage gaps have grown: in Poland, the minimum wage is €410 per month; in Romania, €218. The "European social model" that is constantly talked about by the political class will soon be a reality. It is being constructed right now—on the backs of the people at the bottom. As the economist Olivier Berruyer points out, gaps in wages increase as Europe grows larger.[16] The alignment of minimum-wage scales from below, using the lowest member-country wage as a baseline, will continue. The signing of a free-trade treaty with Ukraine, for example, is excellent news for employers: the minimum wage there is about €50 a month. With the entry of Turkey into Europe (and perhaps then Morocco), one may imagine the European minimum wage being recalibrated with reference to the Chinese minimum wage, rising perhaps to a level of €250 per month. The good news, at least for European workers, is that the going rate is going up!

The working class understands very well what is going on. As the room for maneuver of EU member states grows smaller, it is less and less likely that a remedy for its current predicament will come from a powerless political class. Empty sloganeering by the new bourgeoisie ("Finance is the enemy!") will not much longer put off the day when this class is finally kicked out. The problem is that, in the meantime, faith in the virtues of democracy is declining among the French working class and among the young generally. In April 2016, the global market and opinion research firm Ipsos reported that the growing mistrust of politicians and the media had produced an ominous demographic rift: whereas nearly 80 percent of executives and people over the age of sixty-five felt that "the democratic regime is irreplaceable, that it is the best possible system," nearly 40 percent of young people, workers, and low-wage employees in France believed that "other political systems may be as good as democracy."[17]

Globalization and the facile promise of progress for all that accompanies it are now running up against the hard reality of working-class experience. Globalization has led, not to the birth of a "new man," but to the resurgence of Orwell's "ordinary man." Ordinary men and women are no longer willing to go on performing in the political circus they grew up with. Resistance has ceased to take the form of directed protest; instead ordinary men and women are now determined to take personal responsibility for dealing with the challenges of day-to-day existence. This is exactly what the dominant classes fear most. For if the working class no longer recognizes the authority of the system's elected representatives, no longer subscribes to the mythology of economic and social progress, then it is the very domination of the dominant classes that is called into question. The twilight of the French elites now dawns at last.

No longer believing that the benefits of globalization will be equitably distributed, and still less that upward social mobility will be universal, the working class has dedicated itself to the cause of self-preservation—to protecting and increasing its private stock of social and cultural capital. Its members no longer count on the state to provide a safety net. From peripheral France to the banlieues, they now count on themselves to build a countersociety that will provide the decent way of life that the present system has denied them.

Sovereignism from Below

Globalization and multiculturalism, far from giving birth to a shiny, new, unified world, have brought forth an impoverished and embattled society. If the level of racist violence (with the exception of antisemitic acts)[18] remains relatively low in France, at least by comparison with Great Britain, the Netherlands, Germany, and, of course, the United States, cultural tensions and the identitarian impulses ("paranoia") to which they give rise are all but inevitable in a country that recognizes neither ethnic communities nor national origins. The political class disclaims all responsibility, taking cover behind a moral and/or republican façade in order to stereotype the members of the working class as racist (even inbred) "poor whites"[19] and victimized (sometimes Islamized) "poor Arabs" and "poor blacks."

In the meantime the working class has had to come to terms with the clash of cultural identities on a budget of €1,000 a month. Daily life under these circumstances requires facing up to real complexities, not the false simplicities of ideology. It contradicts on every point the soothing reassurances dispensed by the dominant classes, which continue to advertise the pacifying properties of a multiculturalism that they themselves manage to avoid living with. According to the official version, there are two options: social integration or civil war. But what if reality were more complicated than that? What if one were to grant that the working poor are capable of making a more subtle diagnosis of their relationship to people whose situation is different from theirs? What makes the problem of identity so intractable is not that the people of peripheral France think about it the wrong way, but that they are obliged to endure a life of social and cultural insecurity under a system they have not freely chosen. At its present level, a certain degree of ambivalence on all sides is only to be expected.

The embrace of identity by members of the working class, regardless of ethnic or national origin, is a natural response to a model of society that the dominant classes have chosen and imposed on them against their will. The idea that the most disadvantaged members of society are somehow inherently violent is absurd on its face. Confronted with a system that robs them of security, their primary interest is not in provoking confrontation but in protecting themselves—which means working to preserve their social and cultural capital. The assertion of identity in all working-class settings today has a long history that cannot be squared with the received view. Politicians and journalists maintain that the members of the working class, because they are childlike and therefore easily manipulated, are naturally attracted to loathsome ideologies that gratify their base instincts; having drunk from the poisoned fountains of "populism" and "Islamicism," they are now preparing for civil war. Putting to one side the specific question of Islamist radicalization,[20] however, it will be clear that the most disadvantaged seek above all to protect the social networks on which they chiefly depend.

Identitarian impulses spring not from ideology, then, but from globalization, changing patterns of territorial organization, intensifying flows of immigration, and the unrepresentativeness of the political class. The mounting pressures of everyday life have fundamentally altered the character of society, starting at the bottom. For several decades now cultural separatism has taken root and flourished, driving a fatal wedge between working-class France and the French elites. The political analysis peddled by the dominant classes is now obsolete and moribund.

From the Dream of Togetherness to the Reality of Separation

"The solution," according to the Socialist mayor of the ethnically mixed Paris suburb of Sarcelles, François Pupponi, "would be social and ethnic diversity in all neighborhoods, but France has been trying for thirty years now and hasn't succeeded."[21] The distance between the conciliatory promises of the dominant classes and the wholly contradictory reality of working-class life explains why it is impossible to form a favorable judgment of the effectiveness of municipal public policy, particularly in connection with the banlieues. Even if, technically, urban policy may have been a success, on balance, considering its stated objective of achieving social (read: "ethnic") diversity, it can only be considered a failure. Whatever benefits ethnic diversity may have yielded were bound to be overshadowed by the uncertainties experienced on a daily basis by people who are primarily concerned with enriching social networks of reciprocity, trust, and cooperation—their last line of defense in coping with events that otherwise would be beyond their control altogether.

We saw earlier that the campaign to persuade whites to come back to majority Arab or black neighborhoods has done nothing to arrest the process of racial concentration. The fact that urban-renewal projects have not succeeded in restoring ethnocultural balance in these places does not mean, of course, that socioeconomic diversity is nonexistent there; to the contrary, these neighborhoods do produce new members of the middle class in the traditional sense, which is to say young university graduates from upwardly mobile households. Although a part of this population moves elsewhere, some stay or else buy homes not far from the neighborhoods or communities they grew up in. When property ownership in a given neighborhood is encouraged as a matter of municipal policy, homes are typically purchased by people already living there who fit the dominant ethnic and/or cultural profile. Again, there is nothing very surprising about this. People in the banlieues, no less than in working-class neighborhoods in other parts of peripheral France, are understandably inclined to try to perpetuate existing networks of family and friends by remaining in places that favor the preservation of social ties. The sociologist Christine Lelévrier has shown that, contrary to what is usually supposed, rootedness in a local community is a valuable resource for poor households.[22] These neighborhoods are not, or not only, places to which people have been relegated; they are also places of opportunity and advancement. For apart from the specific benefits that people who choose to stay may enjoy (a home improvement, for example, or actually a new and better home), the neighborhoods in which they live were, and continue to be, net assets because they provide access to social networks and the advantages that these networks create. It needs to be kept in mind, too, that bringing people from different social groups together has never been an objective of the working class itself. Workers' neighborhoods did not used to be mixed. But that did not stand in the way of economic integration or prevent upward social mobility for at least some members of the working class. The fundamental thing from their point of view, as I say, is preserving and adding to a stock of social and cultural capital that strengthens social ties and, in the best case, promotes a spirit of mutual aid. That they should wish to live together with people whose income and stock of social and cultural capital are roughly equivalent to theirs makes perfect sense.

The concept of empowerment gained currency in the United States more than fifty years ago, originally in connection with the civil rights movement, as a way of creating a sense of community and initiative among people who had been left behind. It also suggested a way to oppose regressive government policies while at the same time responding to the skepticism of those who saw no point in becoming politically involved. It held out the prospect of cooperation among individuals and civic associations for the purpose of improving social and economic conditions and raising living standards. Participatory democracy of this kind is all very well and good, I say nothing against it. But it offers little or no hope of dismantling a power structure controlled by politicians and their wealthy sponsors.

The working class today seeks a different kind of empowerment, a way of using one or another sort of identity to find a way out from social and political oppression. In the banlieues, it assumes the form of religion; elsewhere in peripheral France, of cultural reaffirmation and reinvestment in the "village."[23] In each case the process is the same; in neither case does it preclude openness to others. "The universal," as the Portuguese poet Miguel Torga put it, "is the local minus the walls."[24] This attachment to a particular place—sovereignism from below, as it may be called—is common to the working class as a whole, regardless of ethnic or national origin.

Sovereignism as a Self-Protective Mechanism

If globalism is overwhelmingly endorsed by the upper classes, a clear majority of the working class is committed to sovereignism in just this sense. In peripheral France generally, including the banlieues, support for the idea of a welfare state—for the idea that the nation has a duty to protect all its citizens, not merely a few—is undiminished. The wave of populist feeling that has surfaced in elections in peripheries everywhere (not only in France but in all developed countries) illustrates the broad and enduring appeal of sovereignism as a counterbalance to globalization. The working poor of the banlieues, though they do not belong to populist parties that object to official immigration policy, are no less attached to the places where they live than are the white working poor of the small and medium-sized cities and the countryside; throughout the land an abiding attachment to "villages" is expressed by a solemn reverence for the ancestral home of one's parents and grandparents and for its national flag. Regardless of ethnic origin, the members of the working class are resolved to defend exactly those ancient and innocent sentiments that the dominant classes condemn as racist and fascist. Having rid themselves of traditional political allegiances, they are now in the process of reinvesting their social and cultural capital. I repeat yet again: this is not the sign of an irrational retreat from the world; it is a rational response to a neoliberal global model that destroys all sense of community.

The political class is well aware that the ground has shifted. For quite a while now the major parties have taken the problem of identity into account in marketing their candidates to voters. Jérôme Fourquet, a director of studies at the French Institute of Public Opinion (IFOP), is not alone in noting that the motivations of working-class voters are now considered to be essentially ethnocultural.[25] "Society does not exist," Margaret Thatcher was fond of saying in the

1980s. To this the dominant classes would add today: the social question does not exist either.

The dynamic of separatism operating within the working class as a response to cultural insecurity was first set in motion three decades ago.[26] By now it has redrawn the social and cultural geography of the entire country.

Separatism and Antisemitism

The phenomenon of separatism illuminates the chasm that has opened up between the ideology of the higher France and the reality of everyday life in the lower France. What impact, for example, can policies promoting diversity have in a suburb such as Sarcelles, where ethnocultural tensions have erupted into sectarian violence, notably in July 2014 with attacks on Jewish-owned businesses and a synagogue? The displacement of the Jewish population in and around Paris is revelatory of the strains that are felt in French society as a whole. Living together now increasingly means living apart. The historian Georges Bensoussan, who contributed an essay to a volume about antisemitism, racism, and sexism in French schools that was published some fifteen years ago,[27] recently recalled that many of his fellow contributors "were paralyzed at the thought of mentioning anti-white or anti-French racism."[28] Times have changed. The growth of separatist feeling among the lower classes today comes at a moment when the balance of minorities and majorities is constantly in flux.

The departure of Jews from areas like Seine-Saint-Denis, northeast of Paris, and from troubled neighborhoods with large immigrant populations from North and sub-Saharan Africa is a striking example. In Europe today, as in Muslim countries, Jews form a structurally minority community that depends on the goodwill of the majority.

Contemporary Jewish history in France can therefore be seen not as an isolated experience but as an instance of a quite general phenomenon. This means ignoring the self-appointed spokespersons from the intellectual class and taking seriously the keen sense of resentment that is widespread in working-class Jewish communities. Georges Bensoussan has shown that Muslim-Jewish relations in North Africa (70 percent of French Jews are Sephardi) evolved during the nineteenth and twentieth centuries as a function of class position and daily experience.[29] Working-class Jews in North Africa did not have the same experience as the Jewish bourgeoisie. Whereas the relationship to Muslims was primarily a class relation for middle-class Jews, it was a much more complicated matter for members of the lower class. Poorer Jews, though they had to confront a form of what Bensoussan calls traditional antisemitism, were not therefore prevented from developing common interests with Arabs. Cultural difference in working-class settings typically assumed the form of an ambivalent and complex relationship in which the same person might be hostile in the morning and friendly in the afternoon. But as rejection by the Arab majority became more pronounced over time, Jews gradually withdrew from communities where they had long lived. The same pattern of behavior has been observed recently in France, where an increase in the number of antisemitic acts in predominantly Muslim immigrant neighborhoods has typically led to the departure of Jewish working-class residents.

The political scientist Jérôme Fourquet and the geographer Sylvain Manternach have analyzed the flight of Jews during the past fifteen years from banlieues in Seine-Saint-Denis (including Saint-Denis, La Courneuve, Aubervilliers, Stains, Pierrefitte-sur-Seine, Trappes, Aulnay-sous-Bois, and Le Blanc-Mesnil).[30] Culturally mixed middle schools, particularly to the east of Paris, have witnessed an exodus of Jewish pupils. It is estimated that a third of young Jews now attend private Jewish schools; another third is enrolled in secular public schools, generally in wealthy areas, and the last third in private Catholic schools. Politicians and journalists usually interpret this situation in the light of the Israeli-Palestinian conflict and the impact of exceptional events such as the attacks on Jewish communities in Toulouse and Paris.[31] There can be no doubt that events of this sort have intensified tensions. But the nasty looks, the insults, and occasionally the physical assaults that are an inescapable part of everyday life have had a much greater influence overall.

Over the past fifteen years, the departure of Jews from ethnically mixed neighborhoods to places where the immigrant population is small (such as the seventeenth arrondissement in Paris and the commune of Saint-Mandé in the Val-de-Marne, east of the city) and to wealthy neighborhoods and suburbs (the sixteenth arrondissement, Boulogne, Levallois, Neuilly-sur-Seine) has accelerated. It has been further enlarged by an increasing rate of emigration abroad and above all to Israel (in 2016, the Jewish Agency estimated the number of Jews moving there to be ten thousand). Bensoussan sees this as the beginning of the end: forty-seven thousand Jews left France for Israel between 2000 and 2015, or about 10 percent of the community in fifteen years; between 2013 and 2015, the number reached twenty thousand. In both 2014 and 2015, France ranked first among all countries from which Jews returned to their ancestral homeland. Swelling the tide of expatriation still further are the young families and active members of the labor force who are leaving for the United States, Canada, England, and Australia, raising the average age of the remaining Jewish population in France. This dynamic yields a demographic portrait of a community that in the years to come will consist increasingly of parents who have not gone elsewhere and of children who have.[32]

No Way Out

Areas with large concentrations of recent immigrants, the so-called sensitive urban zones (ZUS),[33] are characterized by substantial demographic instability and high levels of social tension. Because residential mobility is very great in these places, the relative balance of minorities and majorities is constantly shifting, and cultural insecurity affects all inhabitants, regardless of ethnic or national origin. Ethnically French members of the working class and members of assimilated immigrant families have long avoided (or long ago left) these areas, with the result that relations between established residents (for the most part second-generation French citizens of North African descent) and recent arrivals (for the most part Romanies and immigrants from sub-Saharan Africa) are now increasingly strained. These tensions explain the patterns of residential avoidance (mainly within public housing projects) and the preference for separate schooling that are now observed among an older generation of upwardly mobile North African immigrants. The sectarian confrontation that is most to be dreaded today is not between poor whites and Muslims but between predominantly Muslim minorities living in areas that they are forced to share.

Tensions are lively also in areas where "deconcentration"[34] is not possible. This is the case with certain islands, many of whose residents have no way of leaving. A majority of violent acts committed against North African immigrants, for example, take place in Corsica, a French island off the coast of Italy. In December 2015, amid cries of "On est chez nous!" (This is our home!) and "Arabi fora!" (Arabs get out!), Corsican youths vandalized a prayer hall and occupied a largely Muslim housing project in retaliation for an attack on firefighters by young immigrants. Racist attacks have been common in Corsica for years. They are associated not only with a specific local context, in which the native population is viscerally attached to a particular history and cultural heritage, but also with a specific demographic context, marked by a sharp decline in the native birthrate[35] and a high rate of immigration, particularly from Morocco.

The question of immigration is also at the heart of violence in the overseas territory of Mayotte, part of the Comoros archipelago in the northern Mozambique Channel of the Indian Ocean, though there economic and social circumstances are very different. In 2015 the population rose from 212,000 to 226,000, increasing the population density from 569 inhabitants per square kilometer to 603 (or from 1,470 to 1,558 per square mile). Nearly three-quarters of the births recorded that year in Mayotte's two islands were children of illegal immigrants, with the result that the native Mahoran population became a minority. Xenophobic acts multiplied, with local observers reporting that the hounding of Comorian immigrants was virtually unchecked.[36] Intense demographic pressures, and the cultural insecurity they are bound to generate in an insular environment where separatism is not a practical option, have brought Mayotte to the edge of what its former deputy in the French National Assembly called "civil war."[37] The situation in the Caribbean islands of Guadeloupe and Martinique is troubled as well. In Guadeloupe, tensions produced by rising levels of Haitian immigration are less severe but nonetheless worrisome. In Martinique, by contrast, the higher standard of living of prosperous immigrants from France has widened social and cultural inequalities that were already a source of local discontent.

The experience of overseas regions and departments makes it clear that the level of hostility between native and immigrant populations depends not only on geography but also on demographic, social, and cultural factors. It is precisely in order to avoid such tensions, in France itself, that people of modest means, when they are in a position to decide where they wish to live, decide as they do. Taken together, their decisions are sketching the contours of a new political geography. The distribution of young adults from the working class, both native and immigrant, shows that separatism is no longer a hypothesis. Over the course of a few decades, the economic and social policies pursued by the higher France will have made separatism a reality, imposed not from above but from below. What is more, the geographical distribution of the working class as a whole makes it clear that the prospect of social harmony is no less illusory than the possibility of resuscitating the old assimilationist ideal.

In a society in which mutual sympathy and understanding among people from different backgrounds is less and less likely, demographic instability is the main cause of separatism from below. Contrary to what politicians and journalists would have us believe, the rate of immigration (two hundred thousand per year, according to a recent report by the ministry of the interior) has been a central concern of ordinary people in France for decades.[38] An Ipsos study indicates that 70 percent of the French today believe "there are too many foreigners in France"; 60 percent agree that "one no longer feels at home in one's own country."[39] Seventy percent is a considerable number—far greater than the best results of the National Front—and long a majority opinion that the dominant classes thought they could sweep under the rug by demonizing it as the attitude of a racist and fascist fringe. They forgot two things: first, that this question preoccupies the working class as a whole, regardless of ethnic or national origin; second, that it therefore cannot be reduced to the number of votes received by the National Front. Do the dominant classes really imagine that so widely shared an opinion has no basis in daily experience? That it is enough to tell people, "You shouldn't feel that way, it's wrong," in order to dispose of the problem? Surely people who have so much experience erecting invisible boundaries in order to avoid living with their social inferiors and having to send their children to the same schools as the children of the working class should have been able to predict that a generally negative perception of immigration would influence not only the demographic composition of the country but also the character of society itself. The members of the working class at least are under no illusion. They know perfectly well that social and cultural separation is a fact of life everywhere in France today. How many votes the National Front gets is irrelevant.

Demands for immigration control are not restricted to France; they are heard in every country (not excluding the United States).[40] No member of the working class wishes to become a minority in his or her own "village"—not in France or Morocco or China or Senegal. These demands are not motivated by racist hatred on the part of a particular ethnic, cultural, or religious group; they are a rational response by self-reliant low-income groups seeking to protect a precious fund of social and cultural capital that is being threatened by the relentless advance of globalization. Fears that the influx of immigrants will continue to grow, and anxiety in the face of the demographic instability it produces, are aggravated by tensions that are the product less of sectarian prejudice than of what is sometimes called identity assignment, that is, the way one regards people whose traditions and way of life are foreign to one's own. At a time when the relative proportion of minorities and majorities in working-class communities is continually changing, relations among people of different races and nationalities cannot help but be fraught. Identity assignment in these communities is something that everyone must deal with, not only "visible minorities." A recent survey reports that 61 percent of blue-collar workers, 56 percent of office workers and other employees, and 58 percent of middle managers in various sectors of the economy consider that "antiwhite racism is now fairly widespread in France."[41] The lasting effects of this view on the political landscape in France can hardly be underestimated. A study by the Center for Political Research at Sciences Po in Paris on first-time voters—defined as young registered voters who were eligible to cast a ballot in a presidential election for the first time in 2017—found that 37 percent of young people from working-class backgrounds and 60 percent of unemployed youth were planning to vote for Marine Le Pen, as against 17 percent of children of business executives, members of the liberal professions, and academics. Le Pen, it went on to note, "is particularly popular among first-time voters from families that came to France from southern Europe (Spain, Italy, and Portugal), thereby creating a political and electoral divide within the immigrant population as a whole."[42] Her party has comparatively little support among young people from North African families: whereas 41 percent of those of Spanish descent, 45 percent of Italian descent, and 50 percent of Portuguese descent said they planned to vote for the National Front, they were joined by only 9 percent of North African descent—a snapshot of deepening identitarian tensions in a country that has been struggling for some time now to come to terms with the growth of separatist feeling.

Separatism has other consequences that are no less far-reaching. It helps to reinforce an already-high degree of social inbreeding through cultural inbreeding. The tendency toward self-segregation among the upper classes, strengthened under the influence of metropolization, not only acts as a brake on social mobility but also encourages social homogamy. The sociologist Milan Bouchet Valat has shown that the mating of people from similar backgrounds remains the norm in France. In 2011, 83.4 percent of male manual workers lived with a female manual worker or nonmanual worker (two and a half times the percentage of executives in the same situation); conversely, only 2.2 percent of male manual workers lived with a female executive or manager).[43] A pair of business-school professors, Pierre Courtioux and Vincent Lignon, extended this analysis by taking education levels into account. The results speak for themselves: two-thirds of men born in 1970 who do not have a university degree live with a woman who has at most a certificate of technical education (BEP); 82 percent of men with a master's degree live with a woman who has completed at least two years of undergraduate education; only 5 percent of men with a master's degree live with a woman without a degree.[44] This evidence of social determinism in both peripheral and metropolitan France rests on the unsurprising fact that most people prefer to live with a person who has a similar way of life, shared interests and leisure preferences, and a like-minded way of looking at the world; more than this, they wish to live in a community in which they enjoy the respect of others.

The demographer Michèle Tribalat, for her part, has observed a strengthening of religious endogamy among younger people.[45] This is standard behavior among young Muslims and increasingly so among Catholics and Jews. Tribalat found that what appears to be an exceptionally high rate of marriage between French persons and foreigners needs to be qualified in view of the fact that many such mixed unions are between individuals of the same ethnic origin. Considering the surge in identity-based demands and, above all, the tendency of recent immigrants to settle in suburban neighborhoods of the major cities with a high concentration of public housing (straining the resources of the welfare state and weakening national cohesiveness, both typical consequences of economic globalization), a return to the status quo ante is very difficult to imagine. Some years ago the American political scientist Robert Putnam detected a clear pattern of deterioration in the

collective life of multicultural cities.[46] In France, the associated wither-
ing of national solidarity will be aggravated in the years to come by the
spread of enforced social and residential immobility among the working class, both in the banlieues and in peripheral France, and continuing shortages of government funding. The situation is particularly
precarious in those parts of the country that are suffering today from
the elimination of many public services while at the same time remaining dependent on the public sector for jobs. It is true that government
policies have made it possible to reduce inequalities in disposable income across regions to some extent. Thanks to redistribution, these
gaps are less marked by comparison with per capita gross domestic
product than they would be otherwise. Public-sector employment has
long been an essential lever of resource redistribution. The relative importance of such employment is greater in peripheral France than in
the major cities because of private-sector job losses and a declining
share of state support for public services. The growing indebtedness
of local authorities and a shortage of funding in general pose a grave
danger to social stability in the years ahead. In many towns and small
cities, the public sector is virtually the only employer.

An Immobile Working-Class Society

The sociologist Jean-Pierre Le Goff, in a recent book on the contemporary crisis of democracy, shows that deregulated market forces
in a consumer society that is dedicated to the pursuit of leisure has
privileged the private sphere to the detriment of traditional forms of
sociability and mutual aid among the lower classes.[47] Le Goff's analysis bolsters the argument made by Christopher Lasch almost forty
years ago, in *The Culture of Narcissism*, that individualism has severed
the roots of working-class culture. All the more clearly, then, do the

most disadvantaged members of society today perceive an urgent need to repair frayed social networks and to restore depleted stocks of cultural capital. Excluded by the dynamic of metropolization, they are now forced to remain in those areas that create the fewest jobs. This form of imprisonment, though it makes their economic and social position ever more uncertain, also presents a historic opportunity by obliging them to mobilize a formidable arsenal of human and territorial resources in new and more effective ways—ways that not long ago were scarcely imaginable.

The Worldwide Sedentarization of the Working Class

To believe politicians and journalists, nomadism is, or soon will be, the new global norm. The idea that "mobility for all" is both desirable and feasible has long enabled them to justify the socioeconomic policies of the ruling class by holding out the prospect of an open economic system—open even to the worst off. How many times have we heard economists tell us that mobility is the solution to unemployment? Every factory closing is the occasion for a condescending lecture to the workers who have lost their jobs, informing them that in order to find new ones they must be flexible, ready at a moment's notice to relocate to more dynamic centers of the economy. It is never mentioned that the most promising sources of employment, the major cities, are precisely the places that have become inaccessible to them because the cost of living there is now beyond their means.

There is a hint of blame in all of this as well, for implicitly these workers are being told that it is their refusal to be mobile that landed them in this predicament in the first place (if you hadn't insisted on staying in a place with no future, you wouldn't have lost your job). This ideology of enforced free-market mobility (sometimes called "movementism")[48] also makes it possible to downplay the growth of inequality that is the hallmark of the present global economic system. The dominant classes do not deny that inequality is on the rise. But they seek to minimize its effects by laying stress on the benefits that workers will enjoy by being willing to move from one place to another, to uproot themselves from areas where jobs are being lost— even if it means having to leave the places where they grew up and raised families of their own.

The fantasy of unlimited and universal mobility is an integral part of the authorized version of modern life. It is assiduously propagated by the media, speaking in a "neutral and objective" tone of voice that makes the idea of a free-floating society in which a happy majority, having freed itself from all sentimental attachments, circulates like commodities at the whim of supply and demand seem both reasonable and inevitable. If a sullen minority, determined to go on resisting change, is left behind, well, that's just too bad.

The myth of widespread nomadism is flatly contradicted by the reality of working-class experience, not only in France but well beyond its borders. Contrary to what the official view would have us believe, most people are geographically stable: they live in the countries, regions, and departments where they were born. In 2013, international migrants (defined as persons settled for at least a year in a different country from the one in which they were born) numbered 232 million, or only about 3 percent of the world's population.[49] In France, as elsewhere, the members of the working class live—and prefer to live—where they were born. Many people do, of course, welcome opportunities to travel and see the world. But they do not want to be forcibly removed from their homes. For the lower classes, relocation is almost always a wrenching experience, very seldom something they have freely chosen for themselves.

Geographic stability is now increasing throughout the world, not decreasing. Traditionally nomadic peoples, even in Africa, are disappearing. The return of sedentism is one of the most significant anthropological developments of the twenty-first century and very probably will be one of the most enduring. Global demographic growth, in combination with territorial constraints, will make population movements everywhere more and more difficult and more and more likely to cause conflict. "At the airports in Rio de Janeiro," the historian Fernand Braudel remarked more than fifty years ago, "a plane takes off or lands every minute. But the travelers aboard represent only a tiny part of the population, its bourgeoisie, no one else."[50] Mobility for all is all the less plausible an aspiration today: voluntary mobility remains a privilege of the educated classes, even in France, whether traveling by plane, high-speed train, or car along the highways.[51] The nomadic world imagined by the media is almost exclusively the world of globalization's winners.

The twentieth-century cult of the automobile—polluting, expensive, and time-consuming—is no longer a luxury that society can afford. In France alone, counting wasted fuel, wasted time, and indirect losses, traffic jams in the major cities are estimated to have cost €5.9 billion in 2013;[52] already by 2010, in the Île-de-France region, the average travel time between home and work had risen to eighty-two minutes a day.[53] It is in this context that the sedentarization of the working class can be seen as a viable countermodel to that of the elites. In spite of the considerable economic hardships that it unavoidably entails, it has the enormous advantage of being socially and ecologically sustainable. One notes with amusement the surprise of journalists and analysts at discovering the attachment of working-class youth to the poor places where they live, whether in peripheral France or in the country's suburban slums. Partly, of course, this is simply the result of an economic constraint, of not being able to move anywhere else; but it also reveals a sense of rootedness, at the level of neighborhood or commune, that is as common among the lower classes as it is unusual among the upper classes.

Sedentism in France

A map of geographical immobility would show that French society remains largely sedentary, undermining the myth of a hypermobile culture of disembedded, deterritorialized individuals. For the poorer classes, which is to say the majority of the population, mobility consists on the whole of more or less short daily trips; relatively seldom is it associated with a change of residence outside the boundaries of the administrative department where they were born. With the exception of the major cities, where residential mobility is characteristic of the upper classes and immigrants, a majority of the population (about 53 percent in 2012) live within a few miles of their place of birth. For peripheral France this figure rises to about 60 percent, as against 40 percent in metropolitan France.[54] The phenomenon has been sustained by an increase in the rate of home ownership in the past several decades and, more generally, by the economic forces acting on property markets that we considered earlier.

Contrary to what one might expect, sedentism is not found only among the elderly but among all age groups throughout the country: a majority of retirees (many of whom come back to the place of their birth), active members of the labor force (typically working class), and young people live where they were born and grew up. This state of affairs is particularly marked in the working-class districts of peripheral France. It contradicts, in particular, the presumed hypermobility of French youth. By far the largest number of those who leave France for abroad or else leave their homes in peripheral France for the largest cities are primarily recent university graduates and/or young members of the upper classes.

The film *Tanguy* (2001), directed by Étienne Chatiliez, tells the story of a young man in his late twenties who refuses to leave the family nest. As in so many French films, the action takes place in a bourgeois Parisian setting, where the decision to go on living at home is seen to be a matter of personal choice. The reality is exactly opposite. Just as mobility among young adults (both in France and abroad) is confined mainly to the offspring of the upper classes,[55] so too the share of young people no longer living with their parents is much greater among children from the upper classes than among children from the working class. The rate peaks at 71 percent for children of executives and ranking members of the liberal professions and drops noticeably for children of nonmanual workers (47 percent) and manual workers (45 percent).[56] There are several reasons why young adults from the working class find it hard to set up their own households. The first obviously has to do with the financial aid and networking assistance that children from privileged backgrounds receive from their parents and the jobs they are able to find on this account, which in turn make it possible to afford independent housing. For young adults from economically depressed areas, finding work is more difficult, almost by definition. The level of education is also a factor: in 2010, 40 percent of young adults without an undergraduate degree were unemployed (as against only 9 percent for those who had gone on to graduate study); in all, only a quarter of nongraduates no longer lived with their parents three years after finishing their education, whereas 77 percent of graduates had left the family home.[57] These inequalities, which grow in proportion to the extent of geographical immobility among the working class, close off access to the most dynamic centers of job creation by reinforcing intergenerational self-segregation among the upper classes.

From Neighborhood Effect to Territory Effect

In November 2015, a government working paper noted that "the chances of upward social mobility for persons from a working-class background (children of manual or nonmanual laborers) vary by as much as twofold depending on the department in which they were born."[58] This is another way of saying that the social escalator functions more efficiently in Paris than in rural regions like Picardy or Nord-Pas-de-Calais.

Île-de-France offers the working class the best opportunities for upward mobility: more than four out of ten children of manual and nonmanual laborers occupy an executive or middle-management position. It is also the region that accounts for by far the most upward social mobility in France as a whole: 20 percent of the total number of those who have gotten ahead were born there. The working paper goes on to say that natives of Île-de-France who live in another region have lower rates of upward mobility than do those who have always lived there. This is a unique case: everywhere else, persons who leave the region where they were born have on average a 10 percent higher rate of upward mobility than those who do not. On the scale of the department, the chances of upward mobility are also quite variable. The share of children of manual and nonmanual laborers who have become executives or middle managers varies almost by a factor of two: only 24.7 percent in Indre and Creuse, for example, but 47 percent in Paris.

Unsurprisingly, differential access to higher education accounts in large part for these discrepancies. The concentration of centers of higher education in the major cities, which is to say in those areas where the supply of affordable housing has continued to shrink, makes it difficult for young people in peripheral France to take advantage of them. Today, metropolitan France has something approaching a monopoly on high-level university instruction and advanced research: two-thirds of the nation's undergraduate and graduate students are found in the largest cities. Some of them come from peripheral France, of course, but the shifting territorial balance puts aspiring young people from modest backgrounds who cannot afford to live in these places in a position that will become less and less hopeful in the years ahead.

It has long been common to speak of a "neighborhood effect" in trying to explain the mutually reinforcing accretions of uncertainty and unemployment in the banlieues. Seldom mentioned is what might be called a territory effect, which nonetheless has become perhaps the decisive factor for the working class today. In view of the dynamism of the job market and the ample supply of higher education in the great metropolitan areas, a young person from a working-class background is actually better off living in a poor suburb of Paris such as La Courneuve than in a mixed rural/industrial part of Picardy, for example, or of Champagne-Ardenne.

The fact that a majority of the nation's sensitive urban zones are located on the outskirts of the largest cities means that they represent an opportunity for young people from peripheral France. While living in a troubled neighborhood is not in and of itself an advantage and evidently does not guarantee individual success, being part of an economically vital metropolitan area equipped with a developed system of higher education clearly improves the chances of upward social mobility. At a time when social conditions have very significantly deteriorated from the point of view of the working class, the emergence of an immigrant lower-middle class in the largest cities offers striking confirmation in this regard. The increase in the number of upwardly mobile households and of young university graduates from underprivileged backgrounds in the banlieues is not the result of a government policy of affirmative action. It is the result of a territory effect, namely, the influence of large metropolitan areas.

There also exists a territory effect—a rather less benign one, however, for the working poor—in parts of peripheral France that have been hard hit by waves of job losses. The correlation of high rates of sedentism in rural areas and small and medium-sized cities with declining social mobility is liable to be strengthened in the years to come so long as young adults from underprivileged backgrounds continue to have fewer and fewer ways of gaining entry to the new citadels of metropolitan France. Indeed, as one recent government report acknowledges, considering the failure of public spending on education and training to reduce inequalities, "discrepancies in individual opportunity from one territory to another are apt to be aggravated." The authors of the report, aware of the effects of sedentarization on the working-class populations of peripheral France, emphasize the necessity of "examining ways to improve the rates of access to higher education through a targeted supply policy aimed at increasing geographic mobility and breaking down the divisions between local school districts."[59] Nothing could be more sensible! Higher education, it will be agreed, is no less an essential social benefit than health care.

France would do well to look to the example of foreign countries, particularly the United States, where many universities are found outside the largest cities. Rather than relocate the National School of Administration (ENA) from Paris to Strasbourg, from one metropolis to another, think of the advantages of selecting a medium-sized city such as Troyes or Châteauroux instead. A bold initiative along these lines could be broadened by moving certain organs of public administration from the major cities to small and medium-sized cities in peripheral areas, where their presence might be expected to create an atmosphere conducive to economic development. The question arises, however, whether anyone is really in a position to bring about such a change in attitude. Some forward-looking measures have been suggested, such as "supporting innovation, making [research and development] more dynamic, and increasing productivity in the service sector,"[60] but they are homeopathic at best. They fail to address the underlying problems (employing, training, and integrating newcomers to the labor force; maintaining existing jobs and helping unemployed workers find new ones; streamlining government bureaucracy and/or finding ways to get around it) or the larger question of the growth in inequality. For the moment, in the absence of a universal basic income, public policy amounts to little more than social tinkering based on slight adjustments and minor reallocations.

Sedentarization in the Service of Working-Class Society

If sedentarization increases the economic vulnerability of the working poor and limits their social reproduction, it has also helped to bring about the formation of a countersociety that instinctively searches for ways to short-circuit centralized policy making and directly encourage economic development at the local level. Looking to the future, the aim must be to devise a new model—not one that will replace the global economic model but one that will complement it.

Here again, the driving force has nothing to do with partisan ideologies and bureaucratic "solutions" imposed from above. Instead it is daily life—the everyday experience of forced immobility, the sense of existential precariousness that is at the root of a profound cultural rupture with the dominant classes—that will cause a socially and ecologically sustainable economic model to emerge from below. Departmental councils everywhere in peripheral France are leading the way in rethinking economic development; a great many of them have already drawn up long-range plans suited to their specific circumstances and needs. I mentioned earlier the "new ruralism" movement that has grown up in Europe and the United States. In France it stresses the assets of rural departments (natural beauty, livable towns and small cities) and the potential for sustainable growth.[61] In order to take advantage of them, it will be necessary to face up to the reality of sedentism. This means that the question of access to higher education in these areas can no longer be avoided.

In the meantime social and economic constraints have helped to strengthen what the new bourgeoisie is pleased to call working-class culture, without at all understanding it. For praising the virtues of "common decency" the philosopher Jean-Claude Michéa has been accused, like Orwell himself, of idealizing the lower orders of society.[62] His detractors do not see, first of all, that it is the reality of daily life that perpetuates the traditional values of mutual aid and solidarity. This is true not only in the banlieues but also in the working-class communities of peripheral France. Ideological conviction is wholly irrelevant. "By what miracle," Michéa asks,

> would ordinary people—the vast majority of whom must to-day manage to live on €2,000 a month [about $2,400]—be able to cope with the inevitable hazards of daily existence (losing a job or being in danger of losing one, unforeseen illness, having to leave one's home as a result of neoliberal "flexibility" policies, flood damage, or robbery, the cost of repairing an old car without which it would be impossible to go to work or shop for necessities, and so on) if there did not

survive, to a quite considerable extent, the traditional practice of mutual aid, of lending a helping hand—among parents, friends, neighbors, and colleagues—that constitutes the very essence of what Marcel Mauss called the "spirit of the gift"? The idea that "the people no longer exist" quite obviously has much more to do with the magical thinking of those who have everything to fear from [the] political awakening [of the people] than from any objective analysis of the real world.[63]

The sociologist Serge Guérin, an authority on aging populations, makes much the same point when he calls attention to the

millions of women and men [who] are obliged, amid a deafening silence, to care for a seriously ill or severely handicapped child, for a companion suffering from a debilitating chronic illness, for an elderly parent. In all there are 8.5 million [such] caregivers, who will not wait for the state to do the job, who devise ways of helping that are close at hand, who form a republic of peers in the sense that they educate and assist one another in coping with shared problems. In so doing they "save" the state, and therefore the population as a whole, €164 billion [almost $200 billion] a year—equivalent to the total annual salaries of all civil servants put together![64]

The members of this invisible republic are mostly people of modest means, people who cannot pay for assisted living for elderly parents or medical treatment for gravely ill children. At a time when cuts in public funding are steadily eroding welfare protections, it is solidarity, not abstract ideology, that has been tried and tested by hard experience and that has a bright future.

The countermodel inspired by sedentarization favors what has been called a "revolution of proximity."[65] It is a response to necessity on the part of the working poor, who have no choice but to preserve their social and cultural capital. It does not herald the promised age of living together in harmony, however. Quite to the contrary: the clash between the global model of the dominant classes and the territorial countermodel of the working class announces the advent of a permanently antagonistic society.

Conclusion

The daily existence of the working class is invisible and inaudible, an untold story of stress, strain, and resistance that cannot be fitted into the mental framework of the dominant classes. It probably will never figure in any of the textbooks assigned in schools or universities. The members of the working class today have no choice but to defy the dominant order by taking back control of their own lives. They are rising up against the economic, social, and cultural constraints under which they have been forced to live, against their will. Far more than either the tired ideologies of the past or their vigorous successor, which has imprisoned the higher France in its new citadels, this involuntary adaptation to globalization points the way toward a world that is now in the process of being born—a world made not by the fine speeches of politicians but by the social insecurity, the sedentarization, and the separatism imposed by the daily existence of the working class.

The dominant classes now realize that they have lost control over the least well-off. The panic is perceptible. The mayors of Paris and London are now prepared to suggest that "truly global cities" emancipate themselves from their host countries. In a joint letter to the editor of newspapers in the French and British capitals published four days after the Brexit vote, Anne Hidalgo and Sadiq Khan praised the dynamism and the openness of their cities, contrasting these qualities to "the lethargy of nation states," seen as an outmoded framework for international relations and a perilous source of isolationist ignorance.[1] In effect, then, the proponents of the global order, who constitute a structural minority in their homelands, have issued a declaration of independence on behalf of the new metropolitan citadels—abandoning the working-class peripheries to their fate as deplorable backwaters. The retreat of England and France from Europe is therefore answered by the retreat of the cosmopolitan bourgeoisie from England and France. And yet, while awaiting the doubtful advent of a new age of city-states,[2] the upper classes will have to confront an existential problem: how is a global model that has been rejected by a majority of citizens to be assured of a future?

Now that the great escape of the working class has gotten under way, the future will depend on the ability of the political class to join them in giving voice to the demands and the aspirations of the worst off, not on continuing to promote an unworkable ideological program. This assumes that the political class will be able to stop denying reality, to cease trying to silence criticism of the existing system, to listen to the grievances of the lower France and take them seriously.

The alternative facing the higher France is simply stated. Either it fundamentally revises a model that divides people, instead of bringing them together, or it must resign itself to headlong flight. The present system, resting as it does on a debt that can never be repaid, is threatened sooner or later with collapse. The great danger is that its overseers will not look past the short term, that they will seek to maintain their class position in spite of the social and cultural chaos the system generates—or else because of it. If the higher France chooses this option, one may be sure that it will do so in the name of the common good, of the open society, of equality, and of the Republic. The true motivations look very different, however. The reaction to the Brexit vote of 2016 suggests that there is a growing temptation to embrace a soft version of totalitarianism.

In the wake of this most recent sovereignist vote against Europe it became clear that the dominant classes are now inclined to recognize electoral results only when these results validate their interests. As in the case of the French referendum on the European Union in 2005, the fair-weather democrats of the higher France are ready to rewrite the rules of political participation on the pretext that the poorly educated working classes do not understand what is really at stake and that they are naturally carried away by their ignoble instincts. It may be a good thing to remind the masters of the new citadels that democracy is founded on the principle that a "dumb worker" and an "enlightened intellectual" have an equal right to decide the future of their country.

Today this principle seems to have been repudiated not only by the elites but also, and more generally, by all those who make up the upper classes. In Britain, in the aftermath of the referendum on Europe, a petition demanding that the matter be placed before the electorate again—because those who voted to leave did not really know what they were doing—received millions of signatures. In France, there were calls for a regime of weighted democracy, with the former conservative prime minister François Fillon declaring that young people should have two votes.[3] In Switzerland, a Socialist member of parliament, Jacqueline Fehr, proposed extending this enlarged franchise to cover everyone between the ages of eighteen and forty. The sudden interest in the youth vote shown by politicians on both the center left and right came on the heels of exit polls indicating that a majority of young people in Britain had voted correctly, that is, in favor of remaining in Europe, whereas persons over the age of fifty had overwhelmingly voted to leave.[4]

In fact, a majority of the young had demonstrated their lack of interest by abstaining.[5] The pro-young/anti-old stance of mainstream politicians masks a determination to establish a restricted democracy from which the disadvantaged would effectively be excluded. Geographic analysis of voting patterns shows that older persons in Britain who voted to leave were largely from working-class areas, whereas the young who voted to stay were for the most part children of the new bourgeoisie in the largest cities, particularly London.[6] In France, under this restricted democracy, one can easily imagine that a notice may soon appear in the *Journal officiel*, the official gazette of laws and decrees issued by the government, of a new points-based system for voting that will assign young members of the new metropolitan bourgeoisie a coefficient of 3, executives and middle managers a coefficient of 2, workers a coefficient of 1, and unemployed persons from small cities a coefficient of 0.5. As for poor retired persons living in desolate rural areas, their participation is no longer required.

The totalitarian wager is nonetheless a risky one, because the global economic model will never be socially sustainable.

Appendix: An Index of
Socioeconomic Fragility

We construct a fragility index using the canton as a unit of measurement. This makes it possible to cover the entire territory of France while at the same time smoothing out very significant disparities of scale at the level of the commune, the smallest territorial division, roughly equivalent to a township or incorporated municipality. In the most densely populated areas, a canton corresponds to a single commune, whereas in less densely populated areas it may comprise as many as ten communes. Grouping together the smallest communes allows us to penetrate the statistical secrecy that surrounds tax revenues and, as a practical matter, makes fiscal information unobtainable for a large majority of the nation's 36,529 communes. The data we relied on are derived from the 2012 census and the schedule of taxation fixed by the annual parliamentary budget vote in 2011.

Our fragility index is constructed on the basis of a group of key indicators that, taken together, yield a socioeconomic profile of the nation's population and the range of instabilities exhibited over its thousands of towns and cities. Eight fixed indicators are examined in relation to the national average. For each indicator, communes having a rate higher than the national average (lower in the case of incomes) are assigned a value of 1. The sum of results obtained for each indicator (0 or 1) gives an overall measure of fragility that varies from 0, for communes in which the rates for all the indicators are below the national average, to 8, for communes whose rates are higher for every indicator. The higher the fragility index, then, the more challenging the socioeconomic environment.

The indicators selected make it possible, first of all, to characterize a given territory with reference to the proportion of manual workers and nonmanual employees, as well as to changes in this proportion between 2007 and 2012. These two categories of the active working population are the most exposed both to new labor arrangements (part-time work and the job insecurity that comes with it) and to the effects of economic globalization (relocation and/or offshoring of jobs).

Another subset of indicators bears on the nature of employment: the share of full-time workers as against part-time workers, the share of full-time workers whose situation is precarious (fixed-term contract, temporary, trainee), and the share of the labor force that is presently unemployed. Unemployment is defined by the census to include all those who say that they are looking for work, whether or not they are registered with the unemployment office. In either case, whether because of job insecurity or of actual joblessness, these indicators describe a socially unstable situation whose impact on households makes itself strongly felt not only as a matter of day-to-day existence but also in planning for the future.

Another indicator concerns housing and, in particular, home-owning households with limited financial resources. Many of these households have inherited their homes from parents or relatives or else benefited from public assistance in order to buy them. The costs of home maintenance are apt to be beyond the means of such households, which may also suffer from what economists call energy uncertainty (not having enough money to adequately heat their homes during the winter, for example).

A final indicator tracks average income per unit of consumption. Particular emphasis is placed on this measurement for two reasons. The first is connected with the problem of statistical secrecy mentioned earlier: we know more about income for France as a whole than for its various administrative departments and territorial subdivisions. The second is that it takes into account the size of households. The number of units of consumption for each household is determined as a function of how many members it has: one unit of consumption for the first adult, 0.54 for other persons sixteen years of age or older, 0.3 for younger persons.

Taken together, the eight indicators yield a composite measurement that makes it possible to isolate and compare patterns across regions, down to the level of the canton. The patterns that interest us involve variations in the size of the working-class population from one area to another and its degree of social fragility. The fact that the indicators combine a socioeconomic dimension (manual and nonmanual occupations and so on) with criteria for measuring fragility means that an area with a high proportion of working-class households will be classified as vulnerable only if its population is at risk with regard to employment and/or financial means. This type of composite evaluation has long been used to assess the eligibility of sensitive neighborhoods in major metropolitan areas for government assistance (taking into account relative rates of unemployment, size and age distribution of families, and so on).

Like any method of statistical classification, of course, this one has its limitations. The first is that it averages data from geographically distinct populations. If the fragility index for a given area is high, that does not mean that all households within it are at risk. A measurement of overall intensity, however, cannot help but imply homogeneity across individual territorial units. A second limitation is that the indicators are overlapping to one degree or another. For example, since the working poor are more likely on average to lose their jobs than are other members of the labor force, the working class as a proportion of the total labor force is correlated with rates of unemployment. The same thing is true with regard to levels of income, since manual workers and nonmanual employees receive the lowest average wages. Unavoidably, then, some households are counted more than once. This would pose a problem if our interest were in precisely estimating the size of the underprivileged population overall. But that is not the case here. What we are trying to do is to characterize socioeconomic vulnerability on a territorial basis and to measure its intensity, which is to say the degree to which the situations of working-class households differ from those of more secure households throughout the country.

To summarize, then, there are eight fixed indicators and one dynamic indicator. The fixed ones concern the following categories:

1. Manual workers as a share of the labor force (23.6 percent on average)
2. Manual and nonmanual workers as a share of the labor force (52.9 percent)

3. Retired members of the working class as a share of the total population of retirees (65 percent)
4. Part-time workers as a share of the labor force (17 percent)
5. Full-time workers whose job security is uncertain as a share of the labor force (11 percent)
6. Unemployed persons as a share of the workforce (12 percent)
7. Annual income of home owners occupying their own properties whose situation is precarious (first quartile < €15,639)
8. Annual household incomes lower than €18,749.

The dynamic indicator measures changes in the relative proportion of manual workers to nonmanual workers between 2007 and 2012 (−5.7 percent on average).

Once constructed for the nation as a whole, the fragility index is disaggregated by type of territory. Here we have relied on INSEE's zoning maps for metropolitan areas while adopting a different principle of organization. INSEE distinguishes several types of area. Urban cores are defined with reference to the concentration of employment and the continuity of the built environment; their relative size is ranked as a function of the number of jobs they support. Suburban peripheries in which at least 40 percent of the active labor force works in the urban core are considered to be economically highly dependent on the metropolis; they are distinguished from communities that are comparatively immune to its economic attraction. The whole formed by an urban core and its surrounding dependent communities is called a metropolitan area. Such areas are classified as large when the urban core supports more than ten thousand jobs. According to this set of definitions, France contains 241 large metro areas comprising 83 percent of the population. Medium-sized metro areas account for 3.5 percent, and so-called multipolarized communes lying between large metro areas account for 5.3 percent. Rural areas, defined as the set of communes subject to minimal urban influence, are home to no more than 5 percent of the population; the number of such communes is a bit less than seventy-five hundred.

Our main purpose in devising a territory-based classification is to construct a socioeconomic profile of the nation on the basis of the demographic changes associated with metropolization, which is to say the concentration of jobs (particularly the most highly skilled ones) and of population in the largest metro areas. From this point of view INSEE's typology is plainly inadequate, for the definition of large metro areas makes it impossible to distinguish between cities of very different sizes. The roughly 250 such areas include not only the largest cities in France (Paris, Lyon, Marseille, Lille, and so on) but also far smaller cities. Among cities and towns of fewer than twenty thousand inhabitants that nonetheless fall in the same category, one thinks for example of Sélestat, Guingamp, Lunéville, Figeac, Lillebonne, Challans, Pont-à-Mousson, Pontivy, Toul, Bayeux, Bagnols-sur-Cèze, Remiremont, Brignoles, La Ferté-Bernard, Saverne, Avranches, and Senlis. Although these cities occupy an essential place in the historical geography of France, quite obviously they cannot be regarded as being in any way central to the phenomenon of metropolization. In order to arrive at a clearer picture of this phenomenon, while nonetheless retaining the framework adopted by INSEE, we refer instead to the sixteen largest metropolitan areas: Paris, Lyon, Marseille, Aix-en-Provence, Toulouse, Lille, Bordeaux, Nice, Nantes, Strasbourg, Grenoble, Rennes, Rouen, Toulon, Douai-Lens, and Montpellier. Together these metropolises constitute a new category, which we call intercommunality.

Assigning a fragility index to urban and rural populations alike makes it possible to characterize the socioeconomic situation of the less well-off in France as a whole. The areas lying outside the largest metropolises make up what we call "peripheral France." Metropolitan France—the France of the largest metropolitan areas[1]—comprises 40 percent of the nation's population, as against 60 percent residing in peripheral France. At the level of the commune, metropolitan France contains 13 percent of the nation's municipalities and peripheral France 87 percent.

Notes

Introduction

1. Ten years ago, the philosopher Jean-Claude Michéa argued that while France was not a one-party state, there was already a "single alternation" in which mainstream parties on the left and the right succeed each other in holding power and promoting the same free-market ideology of growth; see *L'empire du moindre mal: Essai sur la civilisation libérale* (Paris: Climats, 2007).

Chapter 1. The New Citadels

1. Coined by the journalist David Brooks and commonly used in the abbreviation popularized by his book *Bobos in Paradise: The New Upper Class and How They Got There* (New York: Simon and Schuster, 2000).

2. On this point see Michel Pinçon and Monique Pinçon-Charlot, *Les Ghettos de Gotha: Comment la bourgeoisie défend ses espaces* (Paris: Seuil, 2007).

3. Here I quote Michael Onfray, writing in *FigaroVox*, 24 December 2015.

4. See the report published by Ipsos, *Fractures françaises*, 27 April 2016, www.ipsos .com/fr-fr/fractures-francaises-2016-repli-et-defiance-au-plus-haut.

5. The phrase is due to Philippe Muray in *L'empire du bien* (Paris: Les Belles Lettres, 1991).

6. Here and for the figures that follow see Louis Maurin and Valérie Schneider, eds., *Rapport sur les inégalités en France, édition 2015* (Tours: Observatoire des inégalités, 2015). These results were obtained on the basis of tax declarations of gross income, from which the National Institute of Statistics and Economic Studies (INSEE) subtracted direct tax payments and benefits received.

7. See Brooks, *Bobos in Paradise;* also my article "Les bobos vont faire mal," *Libération*, 8 January 2001.

8. See, for example, Xavier de la Porte, " 'Bobos' et 'travailleurs pauvres': Petits arrangements de la presse avec le monde social," in *La France invisible*, ed. Stéphane Beaud, Joseph Confavreux, and Jade Lindgaard (Paris: La Découverte, 2006).

9. See Christophe Noyé, "Territoires de la pauvreté: Les dynamiques de fragilisation des espaces," *Regards croisés sur l'économie* 2, no. 4 (2008): 62–69.

10. See the price index for older apartments published by INSEE, at www.insee .fr/fr/metadonnees/source/s1300, and the information provided to prospective private and professional buyers by MeilleursAgents, a leading online real estate directory, at www.meilleursagents.com.

11. See "Prix des places: La contestation des supporteurs gagne toute l'Europe," *Le Figaro*, 10 February 2016.

12. See Hervé Algalarrondo and Daniel Cohn-Bendit, *Et si on arrêtait les conneries* (Paris: Fayard, 2016).

13. The expression "liberal/libertarian" is due to the philosopher Michel Clouscard, who argued in *Néo-fascisme et idéologie du désir* (Paris: Denoël, 1973) that the leftism of 1968 facilitated and accelerated the advent of liberal capitalism and market supremacy.

14. See Christopher Lasch, *The Revolt of the Elites and the Betrayal of Democracy* (New York: Norton, 1995).

15. Christopher Lasch, *The Culture of Narcissism: American Life in an Age of Diminishing Expectations* (New York: Norton, 1978), 217.

16. This figure and the ones following (with the exception noted) are from the national accounts for 2015 published by INSEE, *Insee première*, no. 1597, 30 May 2016, www.insee.fr/en/statistiques/2121565?sommaire=2387999.

17. See the 2016 annual report of the Fondation Abbé Pierre, *L'état du mallogement en France*, www.fondation-abbe-pierre.fr/nos-publications/etat-du-mal -logement/les-rapports-annuels/21e-rapport-sur-letat-du-mal-logement-en -france-2016.

18. See Gérard-François Dumont, "Régions urbaines, régions rurales," *Population et avenir*, no. 728 (May–June 2016): 3.

19. During the riots of November 2005 in the suburbs of Paris and other cities, some 300 buildings and 10,000 vehicles were burned, and 130 policemen and rioters were injured.

20. These figures come from a recent report on housing and living conditions published by the Paris Urbanism Agency (APUR), created in 1967 to advise public planners on matters of development policy; with regard to the notion of "key workers," see

the two-part study *"Key Workers" French Style?*, published in March and July 2014, available in English at https://www.apur.org/en/our-works/key-workers-french-style-phase-1.

21. See Fabien Escalona and Mathieu Vieira, "Les idéopôles, laboratoires de la recomposition de l'électorat socialiste," Notes de la Fondation Jean Jaurès, 6 February 2012, https://jean-jaures.org/nos-productions/Les-ideopoles-laboratoires-de-la-recomposition-de-l-electorat-socialiste.

22. See the 24 February 2016 interview with Jean-Claude Michéa in the online journal *Le Comptoir*, https://comptoir.org/2016/02/24/jean-claude-michea-ceux-den-bas-apparaissent-de-moins-en-moins-sensibles-a-lalternance-unique-2/.

23. See Pierre Bourdieu and Jean-Claude Passeron, *The Inheritors: French Students and Their Relation to Culture* (1964), trans. Richard Nice (Chicago: University of Chicago Press, 1979).

24. Cited in Maurin and Schneider, *Rapport sur les inégalités en France, édition 2015*.

25. These figures and the ones following are found ibid.

26. This study was reprinted almost simultaneously in *La Gazette des communes*, 25 November 2013, under the headline "Reproduction sociale des élites: L'Inet comme l'Éna et les grandes écoles," www.lagazettedescommunes.com.

27. See Jean-Laurent Cassely, "Comment la bourgeoisie française a rattrapé la transition numérique," *Slate.fr*, 19 April 2016.

28. These figures are taken from the February 2016 issue of *act:think*, a magazine privately distributed by Roland Berger Strategic Consultants to twenty thousand senior managers in twenty-two countries.

29. Dementhon, a graduate of the HEC, founded the peer-to-peer car-rental platform Drivy, one of the most notable French successes in this sector of the European economy.

30. Quoted in *Le Figaro*, 4 September 2015.

31. Florence Augier and Louis-Mohamed Seye, "Le PS ressemble-t-il à la France et à ses diversités?," *Libération*, 19 May 2015.

32. To judge from the number of foreigners who legally entered France during this period, Sarkozy is in fact the most pro-immigration president of all.

33. These figures are from a Harris Interactive poll conducted for the magazine *Médias*, cited in "74% des journalistes ont voté François Hollande!," *Atlantico*, 15 June 2012, www.atlantico.fr/pepites/journalistes-gauche-twitter-sondage-harris-interactive=391195.html.

34. Polls conducted by two journalism schools, Centre de Formation des Journalistes (CFJ) and Celsa, cited in "Les journalistes à gauche toute: Mais de quel système sont-ils donc censés être les chiens de garde?," *Atlantico*, 16 April 2012, www.atlantico.fr/decryptage/journalistes-gauche-toute-systeme-censes-etre-chiens-garde-presidentielle-cfj-celsa-francois-ruffin-330312.html.

35. From the annual report published by the Conseil supérieur de l'audiovisuel, *Baromètre de la diversité 2015*, www.csa.fr.

36. From a recent article about the group, "Décoloniser les arts," *Libération*, 15 February 2016.

37. These figures are from INSEE's detailed analysis of the 2012 national census, *Recensement 2012: Résultats sur un territoire, bases de données et fichiers détaillés*, June 2017, https://www.insee.fr/fr/information/2882311.

38. All this according to the Conseil supérieur de l'audiovisuel, *Baromètre de la diversité 2013*, www.csa.fr.

39. See Michèle Tribalat, *Statistiques ethniques, une querelle bien française* (Paris: L'Artilleur, 2016).

40. Notably since 2003, with the creation of the National Urban Renewal Agency (ANRU).

41. See Christine Lelévrier, "La mixité dans la rénovation urbaine: Dispersion ou reconcentration?," *Espaces et sociétés*, no. 1 (2010): 59–74.

42. See Bernard Aubry and Michèle Tribalat, "Une estimation des populations d'origine étrangère en France en 2011," *Espace populations sociétés*, nos. 1–2 (2015), http://journals.openedition.org/eps/6073.

43. See Géraldine Smith, *Rue Jean-Pierre Timbaud: Une vie de famille entre bobos et barbus* (Paris: Stock, 2016).

44. The phrase occurs in a review of Smith's book, "Les ratés de la mixité dans l'Est parisien," *Le Monde*, 26 April 2016.

45. Quoted in *Le Figaro*, 7 September 2015.

46. In today's international division of labor, the newly industrialized countries, predominantly in Asia, specialize in manufacturing (including the production of luxury goods), whereas the developed countries concentrate on technologies and services requiring a highly skilled labor force.

47. Again, these figures are from the report published by Ipsos on 27 April 2016, *Fractures françaises*.

48. See Jean-Pierre Le Goff, *Malaise dans la démocratie* (Paris: Stock, 2016).

49. See Jean-Laurent Cassely, "L'intersyndicale des activistes en ligne peut-elle mobiliser la France?," *Slate.fr*, 25 February 2016, www.slate.fr/story/114647 /intersyndicale-activistes-numeriques-mobiliser-la-france.

50. See "70% des Français opposés à la loi El Khomri," *Le Parisien*, 6 March 2016.

51. The social media theme #jesuisenterrasse (I'm sitting outside the café) was a defiant response to the wave of coordinated terrorist attacks that struck Paris in the late evening of 13 November 2015, some directed against cafés and restaurants. The hashtag #nuitdebout (up all night) was inspired by the left-wing social movement of this name that began in late March 2016 in reaction to the proposed labor reforms announced by El Khomri. The tag is sometimes translated as "rise up at night," echoing the opening line of the socialist anthem "L'Internationale."—Trans.

52. Ruffin is the editor in chief of the satirical quarterly *Fakir* and the director of the 2015 film *Merci patron!*

53. Quoted in Aude Lorriaux, "Il y a deux Nuit Debout sur la place de la République," *Slate.fr*, 28 April 2016, www.slate.fr/story/117145/nuit-debout-qui-danse-nuit -debout-qui-pense.

54. See Jacques Julliard and Jean-Claude Michéa, *La gauche et le peuple: Lettres croisées* (Paris: Flammarion, 2014).

55. See the section "Les Bonnets rouges" in my book *La France périphérique: Comment on a sacrifié les classes populaires* (Paris: Flammarion, 2014), 53–57.

Chapter 2. An Americanized Society

1. In France the debate over the Treaty on European Union exposed new cleavages within the left and the right. Those on the left who supported the treaty were led by François Mitterrand; the extreme left, together with the Communist Party, was opposed. On the right, opponents rallied around Philippe Séguin and Charles Pasqua; those in favor, around Jacques Chirac and Édouard Balladur. The result of the referendum (the treaty was very narrowly approved, by a margin of 50.8 percent to 49.2 percent) revealed fresh social divisions across regions, with a significant number of working-class voters casting ballots against.

2. See Bernard-Henri Lévy, *L'idéologie française* (Paris: Grasset, 1981).

3. François Hollande, for example, as a presidential candidate in 2012, took his cue from a policy brief by Terra Nova, a think tank with close ties to the Socialist Party, recommending that candidates of the left concentrate on attracting the votes of

minorities. Sarkozy, for his part, following the advice of the right-wing political adviser Patrick Buisson, appealed primarily to lower-class white voters.

4. See Céline Pina, *Silence coupable* (Paris: Kero, 2016).

5. Branko Milanovic, "Les inégalités de revenus se creusent tant et plus, nous allons vers une plutocratie," *L'Hebdo*, 23 June 2016.

6. See Philippe Guibert and Alain Mergier, *Le descendeur social: Enquête sur les milieux populaires* (Paris: Plon, 2006).

7. The category of underemployment comprises currently employed persons (as defined by the International Labor Office) who satisfy one of the following conditions: they work part-time, wish to work more, and are available to work more, whether they are actively looking for a job or not; they work part-time (and are in a situation other than the one just described) or full-time but have worked less than usual during a given week either because of partial unemployment (also known as technical unemployment, due to a firm's decision to reduce the normal number of hours worked in response to market conditions) or because of poor weather. Underemployment is measured as part of the annual employment survey conducted by INSEE.

8. These figures refer to 2013 data collected in Louis Maurin and Valérie Schneider, eds., *Rapport sur les inégalités en France, édition 2015* (Tours: Observatoire des inégalités, 2015).

9. From a report by SMG Insight, quoted in "La moitié des français épargnent moins de 50 euros par mois," *Le Figaro*, 7 October 2015.

10. From Savidan's preface to Maurin and Schneider, *Rapport sur les inégalités en France*. Savidan is president of the Observatoire des inégalités.

11. The number of regions was reduced from twenty-two to thirteen, effective 2015, and a new unit of local government, the *métropole*, was created; the number of metropolitan areas is now officially fourteen, with the formation of Grand Paris and Aix-Marseille-Provence in 2016.

12. See the government report *2017/2027: Dynamiques et inégalités territoriales*, by France Stratégie, 7 July 2016, www.strategie.gouv.fr/publications/20172027 -dynamiques-inegalites-territoriales.

13. See Simon Prigent, "Le logement, enjeu majeur des élections municipales à Londres," *Le Monde*, 5 May 2016. [Exchange rates calculated at €1.00 = US$1.177.— Trans.]

14. Michèle Tribalat, "White Flight," *Atlantico*, 7 May 2016, www.atlantico.fr /decryptage/white-flight-ces-blancs-qui-abandonnent-massivement-certains -quartiers-britanniques-et-en-france-statistiques-existent-pas-2869062.html.

15. See "Pour 50,000 euros, un 'loft' de 3 m2 sur l'île Saint-Louis," *Le Monde*, 25 May 2016.

16. This quote and the figures following are taken from Maurin and Schneider, *Rapport sur les inégalités en France*.

17. Antoine Fleury, Jean-Christophe François, Hélène Mathian, Antonine Ribardière, and Thérèse Saint-Julien, "Les inégalités socio-spatiales progressent-elles en Île-de-France?," *Métropolitiques*, 12 December 2012, www.metropolitiques.eu/Les -inegalites-socio-spatiales.html?lang=fr.

18. See the IAU report *Géographie sociale et habitat en Île-de-France: Évolutions 2001–2011*, 27 September 2013, www.iau-idf.fr/savoir-faire/nos-travaux/edition /geographie-sociale-et-habitat-en-ile-de-france.html.

19. See Christine Lelévrier, "Diversification de l'habitat et mixité sociale dans les opérations de rénovation urbaine: Trajectoires et rapports au quartier des 'nouveaux arrivants' " (PUCA research paper no. 209, July 2014).

20. See "Centres-villes à vendre," *Le Monde*, 11 January 2016.

21. See "Les centres-villes se vident de leurs commerces," *Le Monde*, 12 January 2016.

22. See the April 2015 report jointly produced by France Stratégie and Direction de l'animation de la recherche, des études, et des statistiques (DARES), *Les métiers en 2022*, www.strategie.gouv.fr/publications/metiers-2022-prospective-metiers -qualifications.

23. See ibid.

24. See Laurent Davezies, *La crise qui vient: La nouvelle fracture territoriale* (Paris: Seuil, 2012).

25. See France Stratégie, *2017/2027*.

26. A "new ruralism" movement has grown up in response to the better-known "new urbanism," not only in the United States but in other countries as well. See, for example, the December 2013 report issued by the Assemblée des départements de France, *Nouvelles ruralités*, www.departements.fr/wp-content/uploads/2016/10 /rapport-nouvelles-ruralit%C3%A9s-campagnes-le-grand-pari.pdf.

27. Robinson, a distinguished economist and, already in her own time, one of a vanishing breed of left-wing Keynesians, is quoted by Gérard Horny in "Le revenu universel, une idée authentiquement libérale," *Slate.fr*, 27 April 2016, www.slate.fr /story/117269/revenu-universel-progressiste-liberal.

28. See Michèle Tribalat, *Assimilation, la fin du modèle français* (Paris: Toucan, 2013).

NOTES TO PAGES 68-75

29. Notably the soccer player Karim Benzema and the actor Jamel Debbouze.

30. Curiously, the absence of Asian players from the French team has provoked no comparable show of anger on the part of the Asian-French community, though there is no reason to suppose that they are any less proud of their heritage. However this may be, the Asian-French have never taken talk about diversity very seriously or shown any great interest in competitive victimhood.

31. See "L'étrange rumeur de pédophilie qui empoisonne la ville de Montreuil," *Le Soir*, 7 July 2016.

32. See the second edition of my book *Fractures françaises* (Paris: Flammarion, 2013).

33. Demographic instability is strongest today in the so-called sensitive urban zones, where the rate of residential mobility (which measures the replacement of a population during a given period) is highest. Many inhabitants permanently replace those who leave these neighborhoods. Minorities and majorities are made and unmade as population movements dictate.

34. Jacques Julliard, "Le vivre-ensemble est une blague, une blague sanglante," *Le Figaro*, 4 April 2016.

35. "We have encouraged different cultures [in Britain] to lead separate lives, apart from each other and the mainstream," Cameron observed a few years ago in a controversial speech delivered in Munich. "We have tolerated these segregated communities behaving in ways that run counter to our values." Quoted in "Les propos de Cameron sur le multiculturalisme font polémique," *Le Monde*, 6 February 2011.

36. Quoted in "Angela Merkel admet l'échec du multiculturalisme," *Le Figaro*, 17 October 2010.

37. Julliard, "Le vivre-ensemble est une blague."

38. Here again see Tribalat, *Assimilation*.

39. Quoted in "La majorité socialiste s'engage contre les produits israéliens," *Le Parisien*, 15 July 2016.

40. Pina, *Silence coupable*.

41. Here and in the rest of the paragraph I quote from the 27 April 2016 Ipsos poll *Fractures françaises*, www.ipsos.com/fr-fr/fractures-francaises-2016-repli-et-defiance -au-plus-haut.

Chapter 3. The Management of Public Opinion

1. See "Donald Trump fait plus peur à Wall Street qu'Hillary Clinton," *Le Figaro*, 3 May 2016.

2. According to David Lafferty, a strategist with Natixis Global Asset Management, Tim Cook, Larry Page, and Elon Musk met secretly with Republican leaders at an American Enterprise Institute forum in Sea Island, Georgia, during the campaign; see "Les patrons de Silicon Valley ont rencontré en secret des républicains pour stopper Donald Trump," *20 Minutes*, 8 March 2016.

3. See my *Fractures françaises* (Paris: Flammarion, 2013).

4. See Camille Peugny, *Le destin du berceau: Inégalités et reproduction sociale* (Paris: Seuil, 2013).

5. See the interview with Régis Bigot, "Les classes moyennes font du surplace," published by the Observatoire des inégalités, 5 March 2009, https://www.inegalites .fr/Les-classes-moyennes-font-du-surplace-entretien-avec-Regis-Bigot?id_mot=30.

6. See Marine Boisson, Catherine Collombet, Julien Damon, Bertille Delaveau, Jérôme Tournadre, and Benoît Verrier, *La mesure du déclassement: Informer et agir sur les nouvelles réalités sociales* (Paris: La Documentation française, 2009), www.ladocu mentationfrancaise.fr/rapports-publics/094000528/index.shtml.

7. The thirty years following World War II.—Trans.

8. See in this connection the government's 2011 report on troubled urban areas, Observatoire national des zones urbaines sensibles, *Rapport 2011*, www.ville.gouv.fr /IMG/pdf/rapport_onzus_2011.pdf.

9. See Serge Guérin and Christophe Guilluy, "Les retraités pauvres, un vote-clé," *Le Monde*, 28 August 2012.

10. In 2015, INSEE put the proportion of people living beneath the poverty line in France at 14 percent of the population; see *The National Accounts in 2015*, November 2016, www.insee.fr/en/statistiques/2121565?sommaire=2387999.

11. See Oxfam's January 2016 report, *An Economy for the 99 Percent*, https://www .oxfam.org/en/research/economy-99.

12. Aron famously argued in *The Opium of the Intellectuals* (1955) that Marxism had come to dominate intellectual discourse in postwar France.—Trans.

13. See Louis Maurin and Valérie Schneider, eds., *Rapport sur les inégalités en France, édition 2015* (Tours: Observatoire des inégalités, 2015).

14. George Orwell, *The Road to Wigan Pier* (1937; reprint, London: Penguin, 2001).

15. In April 2016, a German newspaper published previously private financial information, leaked by an anonymous source, about more than 214,000 offshore entities and their directors and shareholders, among them well-known politicians, heads of state, leading figures in the world of sports, and wealthy celebrities intent on evading taxes. Americans were conspicuous by their absence.

16. See "Pourquoi les Panama Papers épargnent les américains," *Les Échos*, 5 April 2016.

17. See Fernand Braudel, *Afterthoughts on Material Civilization and Capitalism*, trans. Patricia M. Ranum (Baltimore: Johns Hopkins University Press, 1977); the original French text of Braudel's Johns Hopkins lectures was subsequently published as *La dynamique du capitalisme* (Paris: Arthaud, 1985). — Trans.

18. These figures are taken from the 2012 analysis by the Observatoire des inégalités, made on the basis of INSEE's 2011 census reporting tax declarations of gross income, from which direct tax payments and benefits received were subtracted, INSEE, *Recensement 2011: Résultats sur un territoire, bases de données et fichiers détaillés*, June 2017, https://www.insee.fr/fr/information/2884434.

19. In *Les Habitants* (2016), a film about the hardships and anxieties faced by the working poor who live outside the major cities, Raymond Depardon brings back to the screen people whom French cinema and television have forgotten.

20. France Stratégie, *2017/2027: Dynamiques et inégalités territoriales*, 7 July 2016, www.strategie.gouv.fr/publications/20172027-dynamiques-inegalites -territoriales.

21. According to the definition given by INSEE, an urban periphery (or "rim") is the set of outlying communities that in addition to the urban core make up a metropolitan area.

22. See Chalard's discussion of this concept in "Le vote d'extrême droite dans l'aire métropolitaine marseillaise," EspacesTemps.net, 11 October 2006, www.espace stemps.net/en/articles/le-vote-drsquoextreme-droite-dans-lrsquoaire-metropolitaine -marseillaise-en/.

23. INSEE defines a large metropolitan area (*grand pôle urbain*) as a municipal entity supporting at least ten thousand jobs that is not situated within the suburban periphery of another metropolitan area. A further distinction is made between medium-sized metropolitan areas (municipal entities supporting between five thousand and ten thousand jobs) and small metropolitan areas (supporting between fifteen hundred and five thousand jobs).

24. I take these figures from Laurent Chalard, "Le populisme, c'est maintenant . . . ou jamais: Petit traité sociologique pour comprendre pourquoi les candidats de rupture n'ont pas intérêt à rater 2017," *Atlantico*, 3 June 2016.

25. See Gérard-François Dumont, "Un meurtre géographique: La France rurale," *Population et avenir*, no. 707 (March–April 2012): 3.

26. See Eurostat, "Just over 40% of the EU Population Lives in Cities," news release, 5 October 2015, http://ec.europa.eu/eurostat/documents/2995521/7020151/3-05102015-BP-EN.pdf.

27. Gérard-François Dumont, "Régions urbaines, régions rurales," *Population et avenir*, no. 728 (May–June 2016): 3.

28. See Gérard-François Dumont, "La démocratie se construit par les bas: Ensemble, inventons la commune du XXIᵉ siècle," *AMF*, May 2016, 18–22.

29. An ultraconservative, nationalist political philosophy associated with the Vichy regime during World War II.—Trans.

30. It is amusing to recall that this slogan of the extreme right was coined by a left-wing Jewish intellectual, Emmanuel Berl, who wrote Pétain's speech of 25 June 1940; see the interview with Michel Onfray, "Mon hédonisme est ascétique," *Philosophie Magazine*, no. 89 (23 April 2015).

31. From an interview with Pasolini in *L'Europeo*, 26 December 1974, subsequently published in a collection of his writings and articles, *Scritti corsari* (Milan: Garzanti, 1975). [A French translation exists, but no English version has yet appeared.—Trans.]

32. From an interview on the program *Répliques*, broadcast on the public radio channel France Culture on 29 September 2007 and subsequently reprinted in Lionel Jospin, *Lionel raconte Jospin: Entretiens avec Pierre Favier et Patrick Rotman* (Paris: Seuil, 2010).

33. The phrase is famously associated with the siege of Madrid during the Spanish Civil War, when anti-Franco forces proclaimed that Madrid would be the graveyard of fascism.—Trans.

34. See Jacques Leclerq, "Les groupes antifascistes de l'ultragauche au devant de la scène," *AFP-L'Obs*, 3 June 2016; also Leclerq's earlier book *Ultras-Gauches: Autonomes, émeutiers et insurrectionnels* (Paris: L'Harmattan, 2013).

35. This state of affairs recalls Pasolini's remark, in connection with the events of 1968, that he felt closer to members of the riot police who were sons of workers or peasants than to student protesters who were sons of lawyers.

36. See Pasolini, *Scritti corsari*.

37. This phrase, due to Jean-Claude Michéa, links neoliberal witch-hunting tactics to the internet adage formulated by the American attorney and author Mike Godwin: "As an online discussion grows longer, the probability of a comparison involving Nazis or Hitler approaches 1."

38. See Frédéric Lordon, "L'impasse Michéa: La gauche et le Progrès," *La Revue des livres*, no. 12 (July–August 2013): 2–13.

39. The phrase is due to Lionel Jospin, interviewed on *Répliques*, 29 September 2007; see Jospin, *Lionel raconte Jospin*.

40. See Simon Leys, *Orwell, ou l'horreur de la politique* (Paris: Hermann, 1984).

41. Quoted in *Marianne*, 29 June 2016.

42. Quoted in *Le Monde*, 26 June 2016.

Chapter 4. The Defection of the Working Class

1. The French word *marronnage*, referring to the flight of runaway slaves, derives from the Spanish *cimmarón* (wild, untamed), a word thought to have been borrowed from the Arawak term for a domesticated animal that escapes into the wilderness. This likening of fugitive slaves to feral animals perfectly illustrates the dread that plantation owners felt at the prospect of a large-scale escape that might lead to the emergence of a countersociety threatening the colonial economic and social regime. It was not the loss of slave labor but instead the creation of a rival system, and the dangers it would pose to the safety of their families, that slave owners feared most of all.

2. These figures are from the OpinionWay survey published as "La sociologie du vote au premier tour des élections régionales 2015," *Le Point*, 7 December 2015.

3. See Serge Guérin and Christophe Guilluy, "Les retraités pauvres, un vote-clé," *Le Monde*, 28 August 2012.

4. See the report published by Ipsos, *Fractures françaises*, 27 April 2016, www.ipsos .com/fr-fr/fractures-francaises-2016-repli-et-defiance-au-plus-haut.

5. See Ateliers CSA, *L'état du lien social en France fin 2015*, 9 December 2015, www .csa.eu/media/1066/opi20151209-atelier-csa-2015.pdf.

6. See Ipsos, *Fractures françaises*.

7. See Serge Guérin, *Silver Génération: 10 idées reçues à combattre à propos des seniors* (Paris: Michalon, 2015).

8. See "La sociologie du vote au premier tour des élections régionales 2015," *Le Point*, 7 December 2015.

9. See Jean-Pierre Le Goff, "Du gauchisme culturel et de ses avatars," *Le Débat*, no. 173 (September–October 2013): 39–55; and Le Goff, *La gauche à l'épreuve: 1968–2011* (Paris: Perrin, 2011).

10. See the analysis by the French Institute of Public Opinion (Ifop), "Le vote des musulmans à l'élection présidentielle," *Focus*, no. 88, 9 July 2013, http://www.lefigaro .fr/assets/pdf/Ifop-Focus-88.pdf.

11. See "La sociologie du vote au premier tour des élections régionales 2015," *Le Point*, 7 December 2015.

12. The campaign was launched in January 2014 by a group known as Pull Your Child Out of School for a Day (JRE), formed by the novelist and filmmaker Farida Belghoul for the purpose of protesting the government's trial "ABCs of Equality" program, aimed at combating sexism and gender stereotyping, which was to be introduced on a permanent basis in most of the nation's primary schools that same month. The one hundred or so schools targeted by the campaign, in Strasbourg and the Paris region, were located in poor neighborhoods with large Muslim populations. In June, the government announced that the program was to be discontinued.

13. In the 2015 regional elections in Île-de-France, a negligible share of the Muslim electorate voted for the Union of French Muslim Democrats (UDMF).

14. The Directive on Services in the Internal Market, drafted in March 2004 under the guidance of the former European commissioner Frits Bolkestein for the purpose of creating a single market for services within the European Union, was finally approved and adopted after substantial revisions in December 2006.—Trans.

15. See Nicolas Rinaldi, "Le nombre de travailleurs détachés en France a bondi de 25% en 2015," *Marianne*, 30 May 2016.

16. See Olivier Berruyer, " 'L'Europe sociale' des salaires . . . ," *Les Éconoclastes*, 1 February 2016, http://leseconoclastes.fr/2016/02/l-europe-sociale-des-salaires/.

17. See Ipsos, *Fractures françaises*.

18. See the reports on this subject issued by the National Consultative Commission on Human Rights (CNCDH), at the commission's webpage on racism, www .cncdh.fr/fr/dossiers-thematiques/racisme.

19. See Aymeric Patricot, "Derrière l'antiracisme de Cantona, le racisme anti-Français," *Le Figaro*, 30 May 2016.

20. On this point, see the report delivered to Prime Minister Manuel Valls by the Socialist parliamentary deputy Malek Boutih, "Génération radicale," simultaneously published in *Le Figaro*, 2 July 2015.

21. François Pupponi, "L' 'alya interne' des juifs franciliens," *Le Point*, 20 May 2016.

22. See Christine Lelévrier, "Au nom de la 'mixité sociale': Les effets paradoxaux des politiques de rénovation urbaine," *Savoir/Agir*, no. 24 (2013): 11–17.

23. See my previous book *La France périphérique: Comment on a sacrifié les classes populaires* (Paris: Flammarion, 2014).

24. See Miguel Torga, *L'universel, c'est le local moins les murs*, trans. Claire Cayron (Bordeaux: Éditions William Blake, 1994).

25. See Jérôme Fourquet, *Karim vote à gauche et son voisin vote FN: Sociologie électorale de l' "immigration"* (La Tour-d'Aigues: Éditions de l'Aube, 2015).

26. Cultural insecurity in this context refers to the resentment felt by residents of public housing, regardless of ethnicity, in neighborhoods subject to high levels of immigration.

27. See Emmanuel Brenner, ed., *Les territoires perdus de la République: Antisémi tisme, racisme et sexisme en milieu scolaire* (Paris: Éditions Mille et une nuits, 2002).

28. See the two-part interview with Georges Bensoussan, "Des territoires perdus de la Républiques aux territoires perdus de la nation," *Le Figaro*, 14–15 August 2015.

29. See Georges Bensoussan, *Juifs en pays arabes: Le grand déracinement, 1850–1975* (Paris: Tallandier, 2012).

30. See Jérôme Fourquet and Sylvain Manternach, *L'an prochain à Jérusalem? Les Juifs de France face à l'antisémitisme* (La Tour-d'Aigues and Paris: Éditions de l'Aube /Fondation Jean Jaurès, 2016).

31. In March 2012, a young French-born man of Algerian descent named Mohammed Merah shot and killed three children and a rabbi at a Jewish school in Toulouse. On 9 January 2015, two days after the *Charlie Hebdo* attack, a French-born Muslim of Malian descent named Amedy Coulibaly shot and killed four men in a kosher delicatessen in Paris.—Trans.

32. These figures are taken from a more recent interview with Bensoussan, "Vers une marranisation de l'existence juive en France," which first appeared in *Actualité Juive Hebdo*, 23 March 2016.

33. Recall that INSEE defines sensitive urban zones as neighborhoods and communities in metropolitan areas that are designated by public authorities as primary targets of municipal policy in view of the unusually difficult circumstances facing the inhabitants of these areas.

34. Urban deconcentration is a process by which disadvantaged households leave inner cities and settle in suburban neighborhoods.

35. The Corsican birthrate in 2014 was three percentage points lower than the national average of 9.4 percent.

36. See "À Mayotte, la chasse aux migrants est le symptôme des difficultés de l'archipel," *Slate Afrique*, 11 May 2016, www.slateafrique.com/669205/mayotte-une -chasse-aux-comoriens.

37. Mansour Kamardine, quoted in "Mayotte est au bord de la guerre civile," *Le Figaro*, 19 January 2016.

38. See Ateliers CSA, *L'état du lien social en France fin 2015*, 8 December 2015, www.csa.eu/media/1066/opi20151209-atelier-csa-2015.pdf.

39. See Ipsos, *Fractures françaises.*

40. See the five-year international survey published by Ipsos, *Global Views on Immigration—Tracking 2011–2015*, 20 August 2015, www.ipsos.com/en/global-views -immigration-tracking-2011-2015.

41. See Ipsos, *Fractures françaises.*

42. See the fourth installment of the report issued by the Center for Political Research–CEVIPOF, *L'enquête électorale française: Comprendre 2017*, May 2016, www .enef.fr/donn%C3%A9es-et-r%C3%A9sultats/.

43. See Milan Bouchet-Valat, "Les évolutions de l'homogamie de diplôme, de classe et d'origine sociales en France (1969–2011): Ouverture d'ensemble, repli des élites," *Revue française de sociologie* 55, no. 3 (2014): 459–505.

44. See Pierre Courtioux and Vincent Lignon, "Avoir un diplôme pour faire une bonne carrière ou un bon mariage?" (EDHEC Business School position paper, 6 May 2014).

45. See Michèle Tribalat, *Assimilation: La fin du modèle français* (Paris: L'Artilleur, 2013).

46. See Robert D. Putnam, *Bowling Alone: The Collapse and Revival of American Community* (New York: Simon and Schuster, 2000). In this and other works Putnam addresses the very delicate question of the decline of trust and cooperation among individuals in societies that have a substantial degree of cultural and ethnic diversity. See also Jean-Louis Thiébault, "Les travaux de Robert D. Putnam sur la confiance, le capital social, l'engagement civique et la politique comparée," *Revue internationale de politique comparée* 10, no. 3 (2003): 341–355.

47. See Jean-Pierre Le Goff, *Malaise dans la démocratie* (Paris: Stock, 2016).

48. See Pierre-André Taguieff, *Résister au "bougisme": Démocratie forte contre mondialisation techno-marchande* (Paris: Fondation du 2 mars/Éditions Mille et une nuits, 2001).

49. See United Nations, Department of Economic and Social Affairs, Population Division, *International Migration Report 2013*, December 2013, www.un.org/en /development/desa/population/publications/pdf/migration/migrationreport2013 /Full_Document_final.pdf.

50. Fernand Braudel, *Grammaire des civilisations* (1963; repr., Paris: Flammarion, 1993), 566.

51. See the chapter on declining mobility and the resurgence of sedentism in my book *La France périphérique.*

52. This figure was calculated by the London-based Center for Economic and Business Research; see "5.9 milliards d'euros: Le coût des embouteillages en France," *La Tribune*, 17 December 2013.

53. See the study by the French Commission on Sustainable Development, "Les Franciliens consacrent 1 h 20 par jour à leur déplacements," *La Revue*, December 2010, www.statistiques.developpement-durable.gouv.fr/fileadmin/documents /_shared/pdf/IDF_cleoec212.pdf.

54. See INSEE, *Recensement 2012: Résultats sur un territoire, bases de données et fichiers détaillés*, June 2017, www.insee.fr/fr/information/2882311.

55. I discuss this topic in *La France périphérique*.

56. See Ministère des solidarités et de la santé, "Quitter le foyer familier: Les jeunes adultes confrontés à la crise économique," *Études et résultats*, no. 887 (23 July 2014), http://drees.solidarites-sante.gouv.fr/etudes-et-statistiques/publications /etudes-et-resultats/article/quitter-le-foyer-familial-les-jeunes-adultes-confrontes-a -la-crise-economique.

57. See Louis Maurin and Valérie Schneider, eds., *Rapport sur les inégalités en France, édition 2015* (Tours: Observatoire des inégalités, 2015).

58. France Stratégie, "La géographie de l'ascension sociale" (Working Paper no. 36, November 2015), www.strategie.gouv.fr/sites/strategie.gouv.fr/files/atoms/files /note-36-geographie-ascension-sociale-ok.pdf. The figures that follow are taken from this paper as well.

59. See France Stratégie, *2017/2027: Dynamiques et inégalités territoriales*, 7 July 2016, www.strategie.gouv.fr/publications/20172027-dynamiques-inegalites -territoriales.

60. France Stratégie/DARES, *Les métiers en 2022*, April 2015, www.strategie.gouv .fr/publications/metiers-2022-prospective-metiers-qualifications.

61. See the December 2013 report issued by the Assemblée des départements de France, *Nouvelles ruralités*, www.departements.fr/wp-content/uploads/2016/10 /rapport-nouvelles-ruralit%C3%A9s-campagnes-le-grand-pari.pdf.

62. See Serge Halimi, "Le laisser-faire est-il libertaire?," *Le Monde diplomatique*, June 2013, 22–26; see also Frédéric Lordon, "L'impasse Michéa: La gauche et le Progrès," *La Revue des livres*, no. 12 (July–August 2013): 2–13.

63. Interview with Jean-Claude Michéa, "Ceux d'en bas apparaissent de moins en moins sensibles à l'alternance unique," *Le Comptoir*, 24 February 2016, https://comp toir.org/2016/02/24/jean-claude-michea-ceux-den-bas-apparaissent-de-moins-en -moins-sensibles-a-lalternance-unique-2/.

64. Guérin, *Silver Génération*, 19–20.

65. See Bernard Farinelli, *La révolution de la proximité: Voyage au pays de l'utopie locale* (Paris: Éditions Libre & Solidaire, 2015).

Conclusion

1. Anne Hidalgo and Sadiq Khan, letter to the editor, *Le Parisien* and the *Financial Times*, 27 June 2016.

2. See Laurent Chalard, " 'Indépendance' de Paris et Londres: Réponse d'un géographe à Sadiq Khan et Anne Hidalgo," *Le Figaro.fr*, 29 June 2016, www.lefigaro.fr /vox/monde/2016/06/29/31002-20160629ARTFIG00322-independance-de-paris-et -londres-reponse-d-un-geographe-a-sadiq-khan-et-anne-hidalgo.php.

3. In an interview simulcast via Europe 1–iTélé–Le Monde, 26 June 2016.

4. See "Britain's Youth Voted Remain," *Politico*, 24 June 2016, www.politico.eu /article/britains-youth-voted-remain-leave-eu-brexit-referendum-stats/.

5. See the breakdown of the youth vote in Anna Rhodes, "Young People—If You're So Upset by the Outcome of the EU Referendum, Then Why Didn't You Get Out and Vote?," *Independent*, 27 June 2016.

6. See the careful analysis by Kirby Swales, *Understanding the Leave Vote*, NatCen Social Research, December 2016, https://whatukthinks.org/eu/wp-content/uploads /2016/12/NatCen_Brexplanations-report-FINAL-WEB2.pdf; also Sarah B. Hobolt, "The Brexit Vote: A Divided Nation, a Divided Continent," *Journal of European Policy* 23, no. 9 (2016): 1259–1297.

Appendix

1. "Metropolitan France" in this sense is not to be confused with continental France (as distinct from its overseas administrative departments and territorial dependencies).—Trans.

Index

Academy Awards, 35–36
affirmative action, 29
altruism: rhetoric of, 17; of the upper classes, 25
Americanization: of French society, 51–53, 72–73. *See also* United States
antifascism: as a class weapon, 94–99
antisemitism, 119–121
Aron, Raymond, 78, 159n12
assimilationist ideal. *See* republican assimilationist ideal
Aubervilliers, 42, 71
audiovisual field: and diversity, 35–36

baccalauréat examination, 29
Bagnolet, 71
Balladur, Édouard, 155n1
banlieues: immigrants in, 39, 43, 83, 91, 97–98; growing unrest in, 50; public housing in, 11, 21, 25–26; public policy directed at, 115–116; religion in, 117; university recruitment from, 29; working classes in, 47, 49–50, 69, 76, 82, 83–84, 100–104, 107, 115
Belghoul, Farida, 163n12
Bellefontaine, 40
Bensoussan, Georges, 119, 120, 121
Bergé, Pierre, 95

Berger, Roland, 31
Berl, Emmanuel, 161n30
Berruyer, Olivier, 111
Bigot, Régis, 75
blue-collar workers. *See* working classes
bobos (bourgeois bohemians): criticism of (as a term), 17; lifestyles of, 12–15, 17–18, 44–45; in mixed neighborhoods, 42–43
Bolkestein, Frits, 163n14
Bondy, 71
bonnets rouges (red caps) movement, 50
Bouchet Valat, Milan, 126
Bourdieu, Pierre, 28, 30, 36
bourgeois mobilization, 47–49; and gentrified metropolises, 48
bourgeoisie. *See* bobos; new bourgeoisie; traditional bourgeoisie
Braudel, Fernand, 81, 131
Brexit, 99; reaction to, 142–143
Brooks, David, 17
Buisson, Patrick, 156n3

Cameron, David, 70, 158n35
capitalism: as enjoyed by the dominant classes, 13–14, 31–33. *See also* global capitalism

Cassely, Jean-Laurent, 31, 47
César Awards, 36
Chalard, Laurent, 86, 160n24
Charlie Hebdo, 46
Chatiliez, Étienne, 133
Chevènement, Jean-Pierre, 23, 52–53
Chirac, Jacques, 155n1
city: INSEE's definition of, 89–90. *See also* major cities; metropolitan areas
civil rights movement, 117
class conflict: escalation of, 3; invisibility of, 16–17, 28, 77–78
class distinctions: blurring of, 75–83. *See also* lower-middle class; middle class; working classes
class solidarity: as fantasy, 42–43
clicktivism, 47
Cohn-Bendit, Daniel, 22–23
Collomb, Gérard, 23
Communist Party, 106
communitarianism, 70
Conseil supérieur de l'audiovisuel (CSA), 35
Cook, Tim, 159n2
Corsica: ethnic tensions in, 122–123
Courtioux, Pierre, 127

Décoloniser les arts, 36
Dementhon, Paulin, 32
Deschamps, Didier, 68
diversity: advocates for, 33–37; decline in, 39–42; in the entertainment industry, 35–38; within neighborhoods, 40–41; new bourgeoisie seen as advocates for, 6, 9, 14, 32–33; rhetoric about, 34–35
dominant classes, in French society, 2, 5–6, 141; altruism of, 25; challenges to dominance of, 112–113, 141–144;
and family background, 28–33, 75–76; growing influence of, 7–10; and polarization of debate, 97–99; self-segregation of, 5, 6–7, 8, 11, 27–28, 31, 32–33, 78–80, 126–127, 134; and social movements, 46–50; as supporters of the neoliberal parties, 104; taxation of, 26–27; and tensions with the working classes, 101–103. *See also* globalization; new bourgeoisie; traditional bourgeoisie
Dumont, Gérard-François, 25, 92–93

École Polytechnique, 30
economic development: at the local level, 137–138
economic inequality. *See* inegalitarianism
education: disparities in quality of, 9, 28–33, 41–42; as factor in residential mobility, 133. *See also* higher education
egalitarianism, 68
elites. *See* dominant classes; new bourgeoisie; traditional bourgeoisie
El Khomri, Myriam, 47, 155n51
entertainment industry: lack of diversity in, 35–38
European constitutional treaty, 110
Europe/European Union, 163n14; French referendum on, 143, 155n1; gaps in wages in, 110–112; retreat of England and France from, 142
Eurostat, 92

family background: importance of, 28–33, 75–76
fascism: as charge against critics of globalism, 95–96

Fatima (film), 36
Fehr, Jacqueline, 143
Fillon, François, 143
film industry: lack of diversity in, 35–36
Fourquet, Jérôme, 118, 120
fragility index, 91–92, 145–149
France: as an Americanized society, 51–53, 72–73; antisemitism in, 119–120; globalization embraced by, 1, 2, 7, 31, 32; metropolization of, 59–60; Muslim population in, 71–72, 120; refugees in, 43–44; urban perimeter of, 85–86. *See also* higher France; major cities; peripheral France
France Stratégie, 65
free trade, 6, 75, 111–112
French Institute of Public Opinion (IFOP), 118

Gates, Bill, 27
Gattaz, Yvon, 32–33
gentrification: of major cities, 17, 18–19, 20, 41, 46–48, 88; and the new bourgeoisie, 4, 12–13, 17, 31, 40–41; in Paris, 18–19. *See also* mixed neighborhoods
global capitalism: critiques of, 77–81
globalization: beneficiaries of, 5–6, 9, 12, 15, 24, 45–46, 78–80; France's embrace of, 1, 2, 4, 7, 31, 32; impact of, on the middle class, 105–106; impact of, on peripheral France, 2, 11, 83, 85–87, 91; impact of, on voting patterns, 104; impact of, on the working class, 1–3, 14–15, 24–25, 51–53, 54–55, 74, 91–92, 101, 112–113, 125; and income inequality, 9–10, 23–25, 44–45, 53–58, 66; invisibility

of losers from, 54, 76, 79, 141; polarization associated with, 1–3, 4–6, 14–15; social tensions associated with, 10–11, 51–53, 67–73, 95–99; and sovereignism, 118–119
Godwin, Mike, 161n37
grandes écoles, 28, 29, 30; and entrepreneurial success, 31–32
Great Britain: soccer in, 22
Greens (EELV), 103
Guadeloupe, 123
guaranteed minimum income. *See* universal basic income
Guérin, Serge, 139

Hautes études commerciales (HEC), 30
Hidalgo, Anne, 141
higher education: access to, 29–30, 134–135, 138
higher France, 2, 5, 6, 142–143. *See also* dominant classes; new bourgeoisie; traditional bourgeoisie
Hollande, François, 35, 78, 108, 155n3
humanism, 70

idéopôle, 27
Île-de-France: income disparities in, 61; working class in 18–19, 27
Île Saint-Louis, 60
immigrants: as cheap labor, 43–45; and concerns about social dumping, 110–111; geographic segregation of, 39–42; hostility toward, 122–124; in major cities, 38–39; from North Africa, 119–120; and public assistance, 72
immigration: demands for control of, 125–126; tensions associated with, 67–70, 109

income inequality: and globalization, 9–10, 23–25, 44–45, 53–58, 66; in metropolitan areas, 60–61

inegalitarianism, 5, 9–10, 15–16, 19, 51–58, 66–67, 77–78, 102; in England, 59; geographic distribution of, 19; growth of, 129–130; in metropolitan areas, 25–27, 61; in peripheral France, 84. *See also* mixed neighborhoods; new bourgeoisie; working classes

INSEE, 83, 92, 160n23; urban and rural areas as designated by, 84–85, 86, 88–90

Institut national des études territoriales (INET), 30

Institute for Urban Planning and Development (IAU), 61

Islamicism, 114

Islamism/Islamization, 71–72

isolationism, 94

Israel: Jewish immigration to, 121

Jewish-owned businesses: attacks on, 119

Jews: attacks on, 164n31; expatriation of, 121; flight of, from the banlieues, 120–121; and Muslims, 119–120

jihadism, 39

Jospin, Lionel, 95

journalists: suspicion of, 104–105. *See also* press, the

Julliard, Jacques, 49, 69–70

Juppé, Alain, 23

Khan, Sadiq, 141

La Cité des 4,000, 40

La Courneuve, 40, 42

Lafferty, David, 159n2

Lasch, Christopher, 24, 128

Leclerq, Jacques, 95

Left Front (FG), 103, 107. *See also* political left

Le Goff, Jean-Pierre, 128

Lelévrier, Christine, 40, 61–62, 116

Le Pen, Marine, 35, 126

Les Minguettes, 40

Lévy, Bernard-Henri, 53, 95, 99

Leys, Simon, 98

liberal-libertarian ideology, 23–24, 27

Lignon, Vincent, 127

Lille-Sud, 40

Lisbon, Treaty of, 110

localism, 102–103

London: metropolization of, 59; real estate prices in, 20. *See also* Brexit

lower France. *See* peripheral France; working classes

lower-middle class: and the dominant classes, 49–50; and the working class, 42–43, 48, 49, 86, 109

Maastricht Treaty (1992), 2–3

Macron, Emmanuel, 43

Madoff, Bernard, 81

major cities (in France): in a changing world, 141–42; concentration of wealth and power in, 4, 8, 58, 61; concentration of skilled positions in, 30–31; concentration of universities in, 29; gentrification of, 17, 18–19, 20, 41, 46–48; immigrants in, 38–39; inequalities within, 60–62; Islamization of, 71–72; public housing in, 11, 18, 19, 25–27, 62; and social activism, 48. *See also* banlieues; metropolization; Paris

Manternach, Sylvain, 120
Marchand-Taillade, Laurence, 71
Marseille, 40
Martinique, 123
Marxism, 78, 159n12
Maurin, Louis, 60
Mauss, Marcel, 139
Mayotte: violence against immigrants in, 122
McCarthyism, 97
mechanization: advances in, 51–52
MEDEF, 44
Mélenchon, Jean-Luc, 35, 111
Merkel, Angela, 70
metropolitan areas: as beneficiaries of globalization, 14; concentration of employment in, 63–64, 65, 66; as defined by INSEE, 89–90; immigrants in, 38–39; inequalities in, 60–62; public housing in, 25–26; wealth creation in, 58–59. *See also* fragility index; major cities
metropolization, 2, 58–60; and the dominant classes, 5, 7, 8–9, 14, 29, 32, 45, 82–83; of France, 59–60; as an ideology, 92–94; impact of on working class, 15–16, 81, 129; and unemployment, 15; of the United States, 59. *See also* major cities
Michéa, Jean-Claude, 97, 138–139, 151n1, 161n37
middle class: attenuation of, 54; and gentrification, 18; impact of globalization on, 105–106; myth of, 74, 75–77; as term applied to upper and lower classes, 82–83. *See also* lower-middle class
Milanovic, Branko, 53–54
Minc, Alain, 99

minimum wage: in European countries, 111–112
minorities: in the business world, 32; in the Socialist Party, 34. *See also* diversity
Mitterrand, François, 95, 155n1
mixed neighborhoods: boundaries within, 41, 42–43; in large cities, 8
Monclar, 40
Montreuil, 69
Mouvement des entreprises de France (MEDEF), 32–33
moviegoing: as upper-class recreation, 36–37. *See also* film industry
multiculturalism: limitations of, 41–43, 67–68; social tensions associated with, 67–73, 102. *See also* diversity; globalization
Musk, Elon, 159n2
Muslim population (in France), 71–72; in Corsica, 122–123; and Jews, 119–120; political preferences of, 107–108

narcissism, culture of, 24
National Commission to Combat Illegal Employment (CNLTI), 111
National Front, 41, 87–88, 95–96, 108, 110; working-class support for, 103–104, 105, 107
nepotism: prevalence of, 31–33. *See also* family background
networking: beneficiaries of, 6–8; and higher education, 28
new bourgeoisie, 2; as advocates for diversity, 6; as beneficiaries of globalization, 11–12, 78–79; class interests of, 98; as concentrated in major cities, 4, 8; economic

new bourgeoisie (*continued*)
advantages enjoyed by, 9–11, 15–16,
21; and gentrification, 4, 12–13, 17,
31, 40–41; self-segregation of, 5,
6–7, 8, 11, 27–28, 31, 32–33, 78–80,
134; and the single-party state,
22–25; soccer as popular sport for,
21–22. *See also* bobos; dominant
classes; traditional bourgeoisie
new ruralism, 138, 157n26
nomadism: among the working
classes, 129–130
North Africa: immigrants from,
119–120, 122–123, 126
Noyé, Christophe, 91
Nuit Debout, 48–49, 155n51
NUMA, 31

Observatoire de la laïcité du Val-
d'Oise, 71
Observatoire des inégalités, 60
Onfray, Michel, 97
open society: illusion of, 27–28, 32, 38;
and the new bourgeoisie, 4–5, 6–9,
14–15
Organization for Economic
Cooperation and Development
(OECD), 29
Orwell, George, 80, 97, 112, 138

Page, Larry, 159n2
Panama Papers, 80–81
Paris: as bastion of the "left," 13;
gentrification in, 18–19; public
housing in, 26; segregation in,
41–42; terrorist attacks on, 155n51
Paris Institute of Political Studies
(Sciences Po), 29, 30, 126
Pasolini, Pier Paolo, 95, 96, 161n35

Pasqua, Charles, 155n1
Passeron, Jean-Claude, 28, 30
peripheral France: as divisive term,
93–94; decline of commerce in,
62–64; downtowns of cities in,
62–63; economic and social
tensions in, 91, 94–99; elected
officials of, 87–88; and ethnic
identity, 69, 97, 113–115; gloomy
economic outlook for, 65–66,
83–84, 86–88, 93–94; growing
unrest in, 50, 94–99; impact of
globalization on, 2, 11, 83, 85–87, 91;
misperceptions relating to, 84–88;
municipal indebtedness in, 65–66;
neglect of, 94; poverty in, 90–92;
sedentism in, 132; unemployment
in, 64–66; working classes in, 25,
27, 45, 46, 48, 49, 83–84, 90–92. *See
also* banlieues; immigrants; working
classes
Pétainism, 93
Pina, Céline, 71
Pôle Emploi, 24
Pôle Républicain, 53
political left, 155–156n3; shifting
support for, 106–107; social reforms
of, 109; working-class
disenchantment with, 108–110
politicians: widespread contempt for,
104
Ponzi, Charles, 81
Popponi, François, 115
populism, 96, 114
positive discrimination, 29
posted workers, 110–111
poverty: prevalence of, 88–92;
remedies for, 67; statistics relating
to, 24, 61

press, the: as corporate entity, 80–81;
as supporters of the socialist
agenda, 35. *See also* journalists
public assistance: working-class
perception of, 72
public housing, 18, 43, 62; in the
banlieues, 11, 21, 25–26, 61; and
immigrant populations, 61, 88, 91; in
the major cities, 11, 18, 19, 25–27, 62
public opinion: management of, 74–75
Putnam, Robert, 127–128, 165n46

racial and ethnic tensions: in a divided
society, 67–70, 102
racism: antiwhite, 125–126; in the film
industry, 35–36. *See also* diversity
real estate holdings: of the dominant
classes, 12–13
real estate market: in London, 20; in
Paris, 19–20, 62; rise in, 16–20
rebellocracy, 47, 107
refugees: in French cities, 43–45. *See
also* immigrants
republican assimilationist ideal: reality
of, 67–73, 124
Republican Party (France), 103, 104
Reynerie, 40
Robinson, Joan, 67
Rock, Chris, 36
Ruffin, François, 48–49
rural France: growing discontent in,
50, 84; marginalization of, 92–94;
positive aspects of, 138; poverty in,
90–91. *See also* peripheral France

same-sex marriage: legalization of, 109
Sarkozy, Nicolas, 34, 35, 108, 153n32,
156n3
Savidan, Patrick, 57

Sciences Po. *See* Paris Institute of
Political Studies
secularism, 53, 68, 71, 73
sedentism: in France, 131–133, 136, 138
Séguin, Philippe, 155n1
self-segregation: of the dominant
classes, 5, 6–7, 8, 10–11, 27–28, 31,
32–33, 78–80, 126–127, 134; in
culture and media, 38
sensitive urban zones (ZUS), 135,
158n33, 164n33; social tensions in,
122
separatism, 67, 102, 115, 119, 124–128;
and ethnic violence, 123–124
Silicon Valley: as model for urban
innovators, 27–28, 31
slacktivism, 47
Smith, Géraldine, 42
soccer: as preferred sport of the
moneyed classes, 21–22
social determinism, 127
social dumping, 110–111
social media: as outlet for protest, 47
social mobility, upward: challenges of,
55, 75–77; factors affecting, 134–136;
in Île-de-France, 134
social movements: and bourgeois
mobilization, 47–49; working
classes underrepresented in, 46–47,
48
Socialist Party (PS), 23, 78, 103, 104,
107; as advocate for diversity, 33–35;
minorities in, 34; in Paris, 13
socioeconomic fragility. *See* fragility
index
sovereignism, 51, 52–53, 68, 96, 143; as
counterbalance to globalism,
118–119; of the working class, 117,
118–119

Stains, 71

Tanguy (film), 133
Terra Nova, 155n3
Thatcher, Margaret, 118–119
Torga, Miguel, 117
totalitarianism: soft version of, 143
traditional bourgeoisie, 12–14, 21, 26–27, 44–46
Trente Glorieuses, 76
Tribalat, Michèle, 38, 59, 72, 97, 127
Trump, Donald, 75

underemployment, 48, 56, 156n7
unemployment, 16, 48, 102; and globalization, 52; and the lower classes, 55–56; in metropolitan areas, 60–61; and metropolization, 15; in peripheral France, 64–66; statistics relating to, 24, 60, 81; working-class perceptions of, 72
Union for a Popular Movement (UMP), 22–23
United States: income inequality in, 53–54; metropolization of, 59; universities in, 136
universal basic income, 67
urban-renewal projects, 25, 39, 40, 93, 116

Val, Philippe, 110–111
Vaulx-en-Velin, 42
Vénissieux, 42
Vichy France: invoked in tensions between rural and metropolitan France, 93–94
Villiers, Philippe de, 111
vocational education, 30
voting patterns: age and

socioeconomic status as factors in, 143–144; impact of globalization on, 104

welfare state: support for, 118. See also public assistance
working classes: abstention from voting by, 103, 109–110; and access to education, 29–30; condescending attitudes toward, 26–27; diminished status of, 5, 12, 79–80; and disenchantment with the political left, 108–110; economic insecurity experienced by, 15, 55–56, 96, 101–102; empowerment of, 117, 118–119, 129, 137–139, 141–142; evictions experienced by, 17; geographic distribution of, 124; growing unrest among, 50, 96–99, 100–103; immigrants as part of, 19, 43, 44–45, 49, 76, 84, 88, 108; impact of globalization on, 1–3, 14–15, 24–25, 51–53, 54–55, 74, 91–92, 101, 110–113, 125; impact of metropolization on, 15–16, 81, 129; job insecurity among, 52–53; party affiliations of, 107; in peripheral France, 25, 27, 45, 46, 48, 49, 83–84, 90–92; private housing for, 17–18; and the real estate market, 19–21; as represented in the entertainment industry, 37–38; residential immobility of, 102, 128, 129–133, 137; sedentarization of, 129, 131–132, 136–140; separatism within, 102, 115, 119–120, 124–126; and social mobility, 134–136; and social movements, 46–47, 48; statistics relating to, 24; stereotyping of, 113;

as vanishing minority in large cities, 18–19, 59, 82; young people in, 108–109, 133. *See also* banlieues; diversity; peripheral France; public housing

xenophobia, 39. *See also* diversity; immigrants

Zuckerberg, Mark, 27